Raising Good Kids

Other books by Louise Bates Ames

QUANTITY SALES

Most Dell books are available at special quantity discounts when purchased in bulk by corporations, organizations, or groups. Special imprints, messages, and excerpts can be produced to meet your needs. For more information, write to: Dell Publishing, 1540 Broadway, New York, NY 10036. Attention: Director, Diversified Sales.

INDIVIDUAL SALES

Are there any Dell books you want but cannot find in your local stores? If so, you can order them directly from us. You can get any Dell book currently in print. For a complete up-to-date listing of our books and information on how to order, write to: Dell Readers Service, Box DR, 1540 Broadway, New York, NY 10036.

Raising Good Kids
A Developmental Approach To Discipline

by
Louise Bates Ames, Ph.D.

A Dell Trade Paperback

A Dell Trade Paperback
Published by
Dell Publishing
a division of
Bantam Doubleday Dell Publishing Group, Inc.
1540 Broadway
New York, New York 10036

ISBN: 0-440-50706-5

Reprinted by arrangement with Modern Learning Press

Manufactured in the United States of America

Published simultaneously in Canada

July 1993

10 9 8 7 6 5 4 3 2 1

BVG

Table of Contents

A Word to Readers

Advice given in this book leans heavily on the belief that child behavior develops in a highly patterned way, and that predictable changes occur as the child grows older. The better acquainted parents and teachers are with these patterned changes, the more effectively they can discipline their own children, or those they are caring for or teaching.

People sometimes ask whether all children go through these same stages which we describe, and if so, whether they go through them in the same way and at the same rate. Actually, the stages are rather standard. Whoever the child and whatever his or her sex or cultural background, behavior changes in a definitely predictable manner. However, each child proceeds through the stages of growth in his own individual way.

Comfortable ages (ages of equilibrium) tend to alternate with less comfortable ages (ages of disequilibrium). Yet, it is important to keep in mind that some children are more comfortable by nature than are others. Some never hit the difficult stages very hard. They tend to be easy to discipline even at the most unfavorable ages. Others, unfortunately, are just the opposite. Life is difficult for them at nearly every stage. As one mother complained to us, "You said my son would be better when he was three, but he was better for only about three weeks."

Timing, too, is an individual matter. Some children, inevitably, reach each of the customary stages a little ahead of schedule. Some -- whom we describe as immature -- are always a little behind. There is a rather predictable difference here as to boys and girls. During the first six years of life, boys on the average tend to develop a bit more slowly than do girls. They tend to walk, talk, be toilet-trained, ready for school, ready to respond positively to the various disciplinary techniques which we describe, a little later than girls do.

In infancy, a boy baby may, on the average, be a month or two less mature than a girl baby of the same age. By Five or Six years of age, the difference tends to be close to six months. (Of course, there are always exceptions. You could have a rapidly developing boy, or a girl who develops slowly.)

When Gesell Institute authors first wrote about stages of development which many children go through as they mature, some professionals objected, pointing out that children are not all alike. This is most certainly true. A developmental approach to child behavior fully recognizes this fact. As Dr. Gesell and his colleagues have been pointing out for half a century, every child is an individual, and every child goes through the customary stages in his own individual way.

Thus, the behavior stages which we describe in this book should be thought of as a guide, rather than a guarantee.

And, just a word to readers about our use of the generic "he." Up till 1960 or so, it was the custom for those writing about child behavior to refer to the child of either sex as "he." Then came a decade or so when feminist editors and writers insisted that "she" be given equal space. Thus, some authors used the pronoun "he" in one chapter and "she" in the next. Others, even more determined, used "he" on one page or in one paragraph and "she" in the alternative page or paragraph. Some hit on the awkward device "he/she."

Now many, we among them, have returned to what to us seems the simpler and less cumbersome use of "he" to refer to the child of either sex, except when we are specifically describing behavior of some particular boy or girl. No denigration of femininity is intended.

Louise Bates Ames

Introduction

L et's begin this book with a discussion of what discipline is, and what it is not. Contrary to popular belief, discipline does not mean punishment. The little boy who told us "My mother hardly ever disciplines me" was wrong. A parent disciplines nearly all the time simply by the way he or she behaves.

Discipline, as we see it, goes on constantly, since it is the way you live, the way you treat your child, the way you conduct your household that provides discipline. It involves your values -- the things that are important to you -- and the way you relate to other people. A parent could provide all sorts of pleasures and privileges for a child and still not be an effective disciplinarian. Or, a parent might punish a lot and still be a poor disciplinarian.

We would emphasize that discipline is a process of helping your child respond in desirable ways by setting up your living situation so that your child finds it easy, natural and comfortable to behave in ways we adults think desirable.

A colleague of ours, Dr. Fitzhugh Dodson, phrased it very nicely when he said that discipline is a continuous and positive process of teaching that goes on all the time.

Now, to discipline any child effectively, especially at the younger ages, it is essential to know what may reasonably be expected of that child. A good disciplinarian needs to understand the rapidly changing behaviors which characterize the different early ages. An extremely effective way of handling a Two-year-old might be utterly ineffective with a Four-year-old. In fact, one can cut it more closely than that. Techniques which work beautifully with a Three-year-old might fail dismally with a Three-and-a-half-year-old.

More than this, however, a parent must also have a good understanding of the child's individuality, and what works and what does not work with that individual child. In order to provide a setting and to use techniques which will work for any given child, even though they might not work for others his age, one must know what that child is like.

And, last of all, something that it is vital to keep in mind if you are going to be an effective disciplinarian is your own personality. Some parents feel most comfortable with one method of discipline, some with another. No matter what some child specialist, friend or family member may advise in the way of special techniques or ways of setting up a situation, if you are not comfortable with this suggested method of handling, it will not work for you.

You, yourself, must feel natural and at home with the discipline you are trying to use, and it must be suitable for your particular child at his or her particular age. Too many books on discipline to some extent ignore the special nature of each child and base themselves on one special method of discipline such as behavior modification, active listening, feedback, or family council. No one method works for every child, at every age, and in every family situation.

Actually, something that is often ignored — how you as a parent feel about life — has a great deal to do with the way discipline will work in your household. If a mother is tired, depressed and frazzled, the best techniques in the world are not going to produce a happy household or good discipline. Some pediatricians, when mothers bring to them "totally unmanageable" children, plan with the mother how she could get more time off and more fun out of life.

Dr. Sanford Matthews tells the story of a desperate mother who came to see him about her unmanageable preschooler. He asked this mother, "Who is the most important person in your life?"

"My son, of course," was the reply.

"Then who next?"

"My husband."

"Who next?"

"Well, I have an old aunt."

The importance of the mother's (and, of course, also the father's) happiness and well-being is one reason why the so-called child-centered household often does not work out. Sacrifice, attention to and love for children are all very well. Some parents figure that the children will be young for only a short time, so the sacrifice is worth it. But, to be the center of a family's concern gives children a very wrong message. Any child is part of a family, it's true, but only a part. Child-proofing your household is one thing. Making the child the major focus of concern, except on occasion, can lead to lopsided living.

Types of Discipline

Whatever your own special method of discipline — and this, as we have just noted, involves almost everything about you, your child, and the way your family lives — you will inevitably, whether you verbalize it or not, be following a particular philosophy of discipline.

There are numerous philosophies of discipline, but perhaps the three outstanding ones are **authoritative discipline, per-**

missive discipline, and what we call (and recommend) **informed permissiveness.**

Up until 1940 or so, many parents were extremely authoritarian in their handling of their children. They made the rules and the children obeyed. What was considered by these parents to be bad behavior was often punished by rather harsh disciplinary measures. Spanking or shutting in a dark closet were very customary. Many parents did not make too many allowances for either immaturity or personality differences.

Then from 1940 on, influenced by the psychoanalytic belief that much uncomfortable behavior in both children and adults was caused by the way their parents treated them, many mothers and fathers became excessively permissive. As one mother put it, "I hate to get up in the morning for fear of the harm I might do to my child's psyche during the day." Parents who practiced permissive discipline tended to allow their children to do almost anything they wanted to, just so as not to upset them.

A third major philosophy of discipline, and one which we have always recommended, is what we call informed permissiveness. That is, you fit your demands and expectations to the child's stage of development. Knowing what it is reasonable for a child of whatever your child's age may be, you have confidence that your demands are reasonable, and you make them firmly and consistently. This kind of discipline differs from authoritarian discipline in that your demands fit what your particular child is ready and able to do. They do not simply come from your own authority. And, it differs from full permissiveness in that although you permit lapses in those areas in which you know your child is not able to perform, you feel perfectly free to make what you believe to be reasonable demands.

So, three things must fit if your discipline (whichever your philosophy) is going to work. Your demands and expectations must fit your child's age, they must fit his personality, and they must fit your own temperament and disposition. Then and only then will you be fully able to provide an environment which will do the most possible to promote good discipline for your child or children.

However the best you can do, it will not all be easy. One of the most realistic comments on the difficulty of disciplining is given by Caroline Zinsser, in an article in which she evaluates some of the books now available on the subject. She notes that,

"This is all helpful advice, but what one misses in most books is a sense of how grim the disciplinary struggle between child and parent, or child and teacher, can be. The real anger, frustration and hurt feelings that are aroused in adults by children's willful behavior are down-played. The accent is kept on the positive, as describing children as little dynamos."

In her opinion, and ours,

"Discipline can honestly be viewed as a long and tiring struggle — rewarding in the end but not easy along the way. When wills clash, there is likely to be hurt on both sides. And no matter how many techniques of circumvention one may come up with, there are bound to be times of conflict.

Children can sometimes gain the upper hand. They can even become so strong that they manipulate their parents. If writers on discipline would offer more recognizable situations, those in which parents feel themselves driven to their wits' end because the toll of daily stress overcomes the best intentions — perhaps we (parents) would have more faith in their proposed solutions."

This mother's criticism of the child specialist and his or her advice is fair. We write, hopefully, about things you as a parent can do to promote good discipline in your household, believing that our advice is practical and realistic. But, we know in our hearts that discipline in any family will often break down. You can only do your best, and accept the fact that some days will be more successful than others.

7

Ages and Stages

Possibly the most useful thing that any parent can know, in efforts to be a good disciplinarian, is what his or her children are like at each stage of development. Dr. Arnold Gesell and his colleagues at the Gesell Institute for Human Development always emphasized that infants and growing children are individuals, each different in many ways from all others, even from his own twin. In the 1940s, Dr. Gesell and his colleagues also introduced the concept that each age, like each person, has its own individuality.

And a quite new idea also introduced in the 1940s was that good ages tended to alternate with difficult ages, ages of equilibrium with ages of disequilibrium. More than that, that inwardized, quiet, withdrawn ages tended to alternate with outwardized, exuberant, expansive ages. Figures 1 and 2 (at the end of this chapter) illustrate these alternations of easy and difficult, withdrawn and expansive.

We summarize here, rather briefly, what we consider the outstanding characteristics of each of the early ages, beginning at Eighteen months.

Eighteen Months

The child of this age walks down a one-way street, and that street tends to be in the opposite direction from the one the adult has in mind. Asked to "Come here, dear," the child will either stand stock still or run in the opposite direction. Asked to "Give me your dish," he will drop it on the floor. Give him a second sock to put on and he will remove the one already on his foot.

Not only does he not come when called, he tends not to obey any verbal command. "No" is his chief word. Interpersonal relations are almost completely dominated by the idea of taking,

not giving. The child of this age does very little to please other people, is almost completely motivated by his own wishes and desires. He is extremely inflexible. "You program him just as if he were a robot," as one mother put it. This may be the reason that just the right techniques work so nicely with him. Negative and uncooperative as he may be, he is at least quite predictable.

Two Years

Happily, as at each pair of ages in the early years, a difficult age is followed by an easy one. Things are much smoother at Two with respect to almost every kind of behavior. Added maturity and a calm willingness to do what he is able to do, and not try too hard to do things beyond his abilities, make for smoothness. A Two-year-old is more confident about his motor skills than he was just earlier. He is less likely to fall or to drop things.

His language is more available and useful to him now. He can tell you what he wants much more easily than just six months earlier. Also, he finds things much easier emotionally. Demands are not as strong as they were. He can wait a minute or suffer frustration more easily. And, his relations with other people are more satisfactory, both to himself and to these others, than they were. He can be loving, friendly, and warmly responsive.

Two-and-a-half Years

Now comes the first big disappointment. (There will be many others along the way, as good ages take their turn moving into less favorable periods.) Almost overnight, your friendly, loving, amenable Two-year-old becomes difficult and demanding, contrary, oppositional. "No, I won't" is his favorite phrase.

One of his characteristics which parents find most difficult is his inability to make a choice, or to stick to his choice once it has been made. This tends to be an age of opposite extremes in which the child tends to shuttle back and forth almost endlessly between two choices: "I want — I don't want."

"Where has my adorable Two-year-old gone?" parents ask. "What have I done wrong?" Actually, chances are that they have done nothing wrong. Their Two-year-old has merely grown. And, as the years go by, parents will discover that any delightful age seems to need to break up (into a less than delightful one), before the spiral of development brings behavior back to the comfortable side of growth.

Three Years

Happily, and just as many parents feel ready to give up, things quiet down nicely. Two-and-a-half loved to resist. Three loves to conform. Three likes to do what you ask him to do and even likes to share. "We" is a favorite word.

The child of this age is no longer rigid, inflexible, domineering, grasping. No longer does everything have to be done exactly his way. Now he may even seem to take pleasure in doing things your way. And, his language has developed to the point that conversations can be both satisfactory and fun. He loves new words, and they can often act like magic in encouraging him to do what you want him to do. Briefly, all can be bliss.

Three-and-a-half Years

And then things break up again. The child of this age seems to pull into himself, to lose the calm equilibrium which made him such a pleasure to be with just a few months earlier. Insecurity is now the name of the game. Boy or girl is insecure in a motor way, may tremble and stumble, fall and falter. Language may be less smooth than it was just earlier. This can be an age of lisping and stuttering, and tensional outlets are often exaggerated. Children blink their eyes, bite their nails, suck their thumbs, even exhibit facial tics, which are of course very worrisome to their parents.

Along with their own physical and verbal uncertainties, many children of this age have tremendous difficulties in relation to other people. There is a great deal of "Don't look" and "Don't laugh." Or, at the opposite extreme, they become upset because you don't look at them. There is also much anxiety about whether or not you love them. Brief as it happily often is, this is an age of great disquiet.

"Don't look at me!"

Four Years

The secure expansiveness of the child of this age may come as a relief to parents fatigued by the insecurities and anxieties of their child just months before. (As this period goes on, some parents might wish for a bit less security and confidence on the part of their child. But, for the most part, it comes as a welcome change.)

One adjective which most clearly describes this expansive age is "out-of-bounds." A Four-year-old is out-of-bounds in a motor way — he hits, kicks, throws stones, runs away. Verbally, he is more out-of-bounds than in any other way. He boasts, lies, uses profanity and, even more tiresome, uses bathroom language. In interpersonal relations, he is as out-of-bounds as anywhere else. He loves to defy parental commands, seems to thrive on being as defiant as possible. And, his imagination knows no bounds, leading to very tall tales which most parents definitely do not appreciate.

Four-and-a-half Years

By this time, many parents have accepted the fact that most children cannot seem to go from one stage of good behavior to a more mature stage of such behavior, without there being a breakup stage in between. Four-and-a-half is another example of a breakup stage. The child doesn't seem to know where he is or what he is doing. Sometimes he drops back to the enthusiastic exuberance of Four. Sometimes he reaches up into the calm and quiet of Five. And, sometimes he seems nowhere — just in between.

Children of this age seem to have considerable trouble distinguishing real from make-believe. This confusion of reality and imagination can

become quite exasperating to parents, and can at times cause the children themselves some difficulty. Many are moving on into a need for exact details about such things as death and illness. Their desire for realism is often too frank and too stark to be entirely comfortable to those around them.

Five Years

As the child moves out of this tentative age and into the calm, quiet and beauty of Five, most parents are much relieved. Five is one of the ages Dr. Gesell has termed a "golden age." (Ten is the other.) The typical Five-year-old wants and means to be good, and much of the time is successful in so being.

Not only is his overt behavior pleasing, his very attitude is gratifying to those around him. "Today I'm going to do all the good things and none of the bad things," a cheerful Five-year-old may announce. Or, "This is my lucky day!" he may tell you as he gets out of bed in the morning.

His mother is the center of his world, and so it is important to him to do things with and for her. He usually likes to obey, likes to be instructed and to get permission. Gone is the uncertainty and unpredictability of Four-and-a-half. The typical Five-year-old tends to be reliable, stable and well-adjusted. Secure within himself, he is calm, friendly and undemanding in his relations with other people. This is a very happy time for many children and parents.

Five-and-a-half through Six Years

By now the rather predictable order of growth will have made itself apparent to most mothers and fathers. Calm is followed by storm, and this period, when the goodness of Five breaks up, can be stormy indeed. Behavior at this age is in many ways reminiscent of that which occurred earlier at Two-and-a-half, except that the child is now bigger and bolder and rather more difficult to manage.

This is an age of opposite extremes — he loves one minute and hates the next. Since Mother is no longer the center of his world — he now plays that role himself — he tends to be extremely egocentric. He wants everything for himself and wants always to have his own way. This tends to be the opposite of what the adult may demand, so there is much rebellion and refusal to obey. "No, I won't," or "Try and make me," are customary responses when he is asked to do something.

When you, as an adult, are having a hard time with a child of this age, it is important to keep in mind that he is having a hard time with himself. And, the age does have a certain charm. There is a vigor, energy and readiness for anything new that, when things go well, can make him an exciting companion.

This good side of the age becomes increasingly apparent as the boy or girl moves on toward Seven. Briefly, between Six-and-a-half and Seven, boys or girls can be delightful companions — very warm, personal, enthusiastic and lively. Their creative imagination is fun to share and they really seem to relish the company of an adult.

Seven Years

Though the child of this age, like the child of any other, does have moments of exuberance, security and happiness, Seven is for the most part an age of very marked withdrawal. The child of this age not only withdraws from argument and combat, he withdraws from other people. To a large extent, he lives within himself. He reads, watches television, thinks about things. He does not in the least seem to mind being alone, prefers to watch, to listen, to stay on the edge of any scene.

Life at this time is definitely pitched in a minor key. Seven-year-olds think that people don't like them, and that people are picking on them. Some go so far as to insist on the adoption fantasy — they are not the real child of this family which has somehow gotten hold of them with the express purpose of treating them badly.

A Seven-year-old is not as belligerently uncooperative as he was just earlier, but certainly he does not respond promptly when asked to do something. His parents will need to steer a rather delicate course between giving him a reasonable amount of understanding and sympathy, and yet not taking too seriously his complaints as to how badly everybody (parents included) is treating him.

Eight Years

We describe the typical child of this age as expansive, speedy, evaluative. He is definitely on the up-beat side of life's growth cycle. In fact, he is all over the place, into everything new. This includes not only new space but new ideas. Since he is speedy, he covers this ground rapidly. Sometimes too rapidly, because with his strong tendency toward evaluation, he often evaluates what he has accomplished and finds it wanting. Then he exuberantly complains.

One of the central features of life at this age is the child's relationship with his mother. The Six-and-a-half-year-old fought with his mother. The Seven-year-old complained to her. The Eight-year-old is completely tied up with her. Now, briefly, his mother comes first. He really tries to please her and watches her face to see if he succeeded. He values time alone with her. This makes her a captive to some extent, but it does give her a definite influence over his actions.

Nine Years

Age Nine, like age Four-and-a-half, is somewhat hard to pin down. It is an in-between age — halfway between the expansive exuberance of Eight and the calm, smooth adjustment of Ten. Most Nine-year-olds are rather on the quieter, more withdrawn strain of Seven, but usually much happier, confident and self-sufficient.

Though not as generally expansive as he was at Eight, the child of this age is definitely expanding from his earlier, strong preoccupation with his mother. Sometimes it is hard for a mother to let go and to fully appreciate that his friends now come first with him. A Nine-year-old is interested in adults from the point of view of what they can do for him, but the relationship itself is no longer paramount.

The child of this age is interested in doing things well, in doing them right. This can be an age of perfecting skills and of real, solid accomplishment. However, Nine-year-olds do worry a good deal, take things hard and may even go to pieces if things, from their point of view, go badly.

If their increased maturity is respected, most behave reasonably well from the adult point of view. There is much less arguing back than just earlier. When a child does not like your directions, he may look cross and sullen but will usually obey.

Ten Years

Finally comes the age of Ten, a wonderful respite before the inevitable tangles of the pre-teen and teenage years set in. Ten-year-olds' own words speak for themselves and tell us why they are such delightful people.

"Every Sunday our whole family goes for a ride!"

"Yes, I can usually tell right from wrong, and I try to do what is right."

"My conscience might not bother me too much if I did wrong, but it would bother me enough to make me say I'm sorry."

"I try to be good because I think God wouldn't like it if I was bad."

DISEQUILIBRIUM   **EQUILIBRIUM**

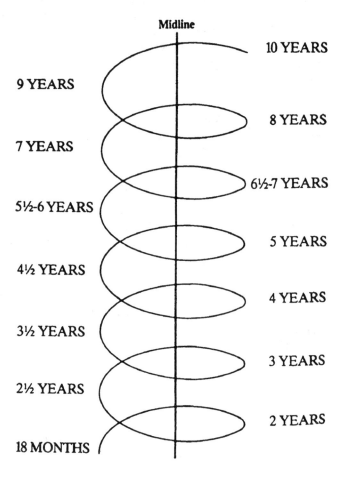

Figure 1
Alternation of Ages of Equilibrium and Disequilibrium

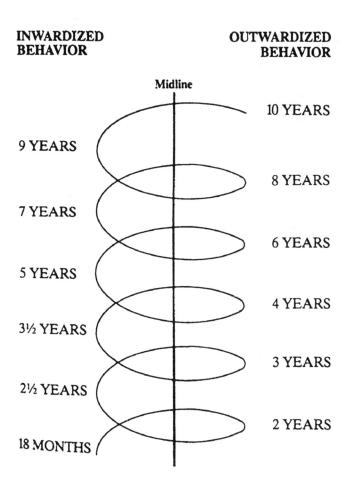

INWARDIZED BEHAVIOR

OUTWARDIZED BEHAVIOR

Midline

10 YEARS

9 YEARS

8 YEARS

7 YEARS

6 YEARS

5 YEARS

4 YEARS

3½ YEARS

3 YEARS

2½ YEARS

2 YEARS

18 MONTHS

Figure 2
Alternation of Ages of Inwardized and Outwardized Behavior

DEVELOPMENT OF EMOTIONS

Infancy:	Stable, well-balanced periods occur around 4, 16, 28, 40, and 52 weeks. Periods of imbalance occur often around 8, 20, 32, and 44 weeks.	**3 years:**	Often time of emotional calm. May be happy, contented much of time. Gets along well with others. Likes others and wants to please them.
18 months:	Acts on impulse. Is insistent, demanding. Not much trouble with own emotions, but has trouble with other people's. Wants own demands met here and now. Not very adaptable or cuddly.	**3 1/2 years:**	Difficult age. Is uncertain, unsettled, insecure, yet is stubborn, demanding, unwilling or unable to give in or adapt. Tends to be fearful, unhappy.
21 months:	More demanding and less adaptable age. Dependent. Has strong needs and demands, but can't communicate them.	**4 years:**	Energetic, out-of-bounds. May go to extremes to test self against others. Often enjoys own impish, humorous ways. May be selfish, rough, impatient, loud. Socially, silly and larger-than life manners may annoy adults.
2 years:	Less demanding. More adaptable. Tends to be quiet and calm. Willing to cuddle and accept affection.		
2 1/2 years:	Great imbalance. Moves between extremes of aggression and withdrawal. Bossy, rigid, selfish, possessive, jealous. Seems to work at being unpleasant.	**5 years:**	Tends to be calm, quiet, well-balanced. Pulls in and usually tries only what she or he knows can do, so is comfortably well-adjusted. Happy, pleasant to deal with. Wants to please adults and is good company.

DEVELOPMENT OF EMOTIONS

5 1/2-6 years: Highly emotional. Not in good balance. Loves one minute, hates the next. Much confusion and trouble between self and others. May demand, rebel, argue, fight. When in good mood, is cheerful, energetic, enthusiastic. Needs much praise, but behavior often merits criticism. This only makes behavior worse.

7 years: Quiet, rather negative emotions. May be serious, self-absorbed, moody, worrisome, or suspicious. Very sensitive to others' emotions. May feel disliked by others and that they are critical or poking fun.

8 years: Vigorous, dramatic, curious, impatient, demanding. Uses words dramatically to express bad things: "This always happens to me." Not as moody as 7, but still sensitive. Very demanding of parents. Easily disappointed if people don't behave as wished. Can be quite critical of others and self. Argumentative.

9 years: Quieter than at 8. Seems to be independent, responsible, dependable, cooperative. May sometimes be temperamental, but is basically reasonable. Demanding of others, but likely to be as critical of self as of others. Very involved with self and may not hear when spoken to. May appear absent-minded or indifferent. Shows anger at parents, but is also proud of them. Protects and is loyal to family, friends. May show concern for others.

10 years: Emotionally direct, simple, clear-cut, usually well-balanced, yet still childlike. Less anxious and demanding than at 9. Most often good-natured and pleased with life. But may show sharp, violent temper. Can be very affectionate. Not a worrying age, yet a few earlier fears remain. Enjoys own humor, which may not be very funny to others. Happy age.

Disciplinary Techniques

Discipline as we see it consists of living, loving, learning; of sharing and caring; of believing and trusting; but most of all of understanding. Understanding what children are normally like at the growing ages, of what they can and cannot be expected to do. And above all, understanding what your own individual child is like and of what works with him or her.

Discipline means not so much what you do as what you are, and what your family situation is like. However, even the best adjusted family does not float through the days, a total picture of happiness. Even in the best run family, children do get into difficulties. Problems arise. Sometimes it is merely now and then but often, especially when children are preschoolers, the whole day may seem like one big hassle.

It is then that parents find that so-called techniques can be real lifesavers, true blessings. "Techniques" is another word for little tricks that, often used almost automatically and instinctively, can help your child or children through their most difficult hours and days. Sometimes they consist of no more than a word or phrase; sometimes they are a way of structuring a situation.

A clever parent often senses what to do on the spur of the moment. But there are many techniques, tried and true, which we have found to be effective. Not every disciplinary problem has to be solved rationally. A good technique can be worth its weight in gold. Here are some of our own favorites.

Eighteen Months

The Eighteen-to-Twenty-one-month-old is easily frustrated and, at his worst, may simply throw himself onto the floor and kick and scream, no matter what you do. In such cases, it is perhaps best either to remove the child from the room or even simpler, if you are reasonably sure he won't harm himself substantially, to remove yourself from the room and wait till the storm is over.

A full-fledged tantrum is the child's way of telling you when things go wrong or when he or she has had enough. Most parents find that the very best way to combat a tantrum is, so far as possible, to ignore it. Even a very young child tends not to carry on unduly if there is absolutely no audience.

Better still is to know your child and his limits of endurance well enough so that to a large extent, you can divert or support him when things are going just too wrong, so that you can prevent the tantrum before it occurs.

One of your very best possible techniques, if a tantrum threatens, is distraction. Let's say you are putting your toddler into his high chair at mealtime and he stiffens out and refuses to fit into the chair and then goes on to wave his arms and scream. Do not continue stuffing him into the chair. Instead, give up this project for the moment. Let him get down onto the floor and then distract him in some interesting way. Do anything which gets him into a good humor and makes him forget that he did not want to sit in his chair and have lunch. Then a second attempt, without any special emphasis on what you are doing, may be met with no opposition at all.

Whatever the problem, you may find that distraction is your most effective secret weapon. Attention span is so very short at this age that many children will go from tears to laughter if an interesting distraction is offered.

It is best, of course, if and when you can, to set things up so that tears and tantrums do not occur. You will avoid disappointment on your part and frustration on his by good evaluation of your child's inabilities and immaturities. Discovering that he does not indeed walk down a one-way street, and that the street tends to go in a direction other than the one you have in mind, you will not rely too much on simple directions, such as the customary "Come here, dear." If you need to have the child where you are, there are several good ways of getting him there if you but reckon with his immaturity.

You can go up behind him, lift him up, and move him to where you want him to be. You will get farther with the child of this age by lifting him bodily and putting him where you want him to be than by talking to him. Or you can hold out a beloved toy, or cookie, or any other enticing object. Or you can turn your back to him and crackle a piece of paper or make some other interesting noise. Chances are he will come to find out what it is that you are doing. There are many indirect ways to persuade your child to do what you want him to. Just try to discover the stimulus that will attract—and there are many.

Perhaps your very best clue to the management of the child in this middle part of the second year of life is not to expect him to do things just to please you.

Most children of this age love outdoors. They like to bumble into every byway, want to pick up every fallen twig. Remember that everything is new to and interesting to the child of this age. Urging him to hurry is not a good motivator. Walking away from him backward for some reason or other makes you attractive to him, and the chances are he will come running.

Out of doors, one of your best techniques is to put him into his stroller and then to go for a long, long walk. Most boys and girls at this age love carriage rides. Many, even the most difficult and least easily satisfied, will ride contentedly as long as anyone is available to push them. Similarly, many are equally content to go for long car rides. In fact, since the out-of-doors offers more opportunities and fewer hazards than does indoors, spend as much time as you can outside the house.

Your Eighteen-to-Twenty-one-month-old may very likely resist being touched or having his arm held (even when he darts dangerously out into the street), but many will accept a harness if it is used only when needed. The harness should be used with loose reins except when you need to pull it tight.

Indoors, the success of the child's play depends largely upon the presence of multiple, even though simple, playthings and the absence of any hazardous equipment. Because the child of this age is a furniture mover and is beginning to be a good climber, it is wise to remove chests of drawers and small tables and chairs which he can move, while he is playing in his room. If a chest of drawers remains, the drawers should be kept locked to keep him from getting into them. Or his dresser could be turned to face the wall. Windows and screens should, of course, be securely fastened.

Toys which are too difficult to handle, and which thus bring on crying, or toys which offer any hazard whatever should be permitted only when adults are present. Books which the child is likely to tear should not be left available, even though you may be willing for him to play with (and tear) discarded magazines. Light plugs should be either disconnected or covered over because of the danger of an electric shock resulting from the child's inserting sharp metal objects.

Since at this age it is extremely difficult, if not impossible, to teach the child to leave things alone and not to touch, you get farther simply by making things you do not want him to touch unavailable. Either keep things out of his reach, or keep him out of hazardous areas. Simple gates are one of your best bets, or locking doors, or putting things up out of reach.

Keep in mind that this is not an age at which you will successfully decide, "It's high time now that he does so-and-so." High time or not, if his body and brain are not ready, you are not likely to succeed. Great patience and a wise assessment of what he or she is ready for will save you a great deal of time and trouble.

Discipline as we usually think of it is not the important thing at this age. It is not necessary yet to make the child obey you in the conventional sense. It is more important, by whatever means you can, to arrange just to get your child smoothly through the day.

In general, you will see that the chief techniques effective with a Fifteen-to-Twenty-one-month-old are rather gross and physical. You control him by con-trolling the surroundings and by just not having too many things around that will get him into difficulty. Or you can con-trol his activity by a harness or simply by picking him up and putting him where you want him to be, without words and with no big fuss. Lan-guage in general is not (as it will be later) his strongest motivator. If you do use lan-guage to motivate him, keep it very simple and use words of one syllable only.

One of the best techniques, if one thinks of it as such, is to permit, without comment, any of the usual tensional outlets which give so much support and comfort to the child of this age. Let him suck his thumb or pacifier. Let him carry around his favorite piece of blanket. Whatever gives comfort is worth its weight in gold.

Actually naps, though they may not usually be thought of as such, can be one of your best techniques. They free you from the child, and they free him from the demands of his own busyness and exertion.

One final thing which a parent might keep in mind at this or any other age. This is that much cranky, irritable behavior can be caused by the child's allergic reaction to something he is eating, drinking, or inhaling. A visit to a good pediatric allergist is never a mistake if your child seems to be continually unhappy and nothing you try either pleases or satisfies him.

Two Years to Two-and-a-half Years

Typically, briefly, and if you are fortunate, when your child is around Two, you may not need to use many techniques. But as he or she reaches the often surprisingly difficult age of Two-and-a-half, you will need all the techniques you can muster. These can, indeed be difficult times but, perhaps surprisingly, children are remarkably alike and remarkably vulnerable to rather simple techniques or ways of being handled.

First of all, we suggest that you take advantage of the child's ritualistic tendencies. Do this by setting up rituals of your own to get him through the rough spots of the day. A good bedtime ritual, for instance, especially at Two-and-a-half, may solve that often very difficult problem of getting the child to bed.

Such a ritual may include first undressing, then the bath, then pajamas being put on and teeth being brushed, then a swing on a doorway swing, then going to the bathroom, then bed and a certain number of certain bedtime stories, then a hug and a goodnight kiss, and then lights out. All of this may seem to take rather a long time, particularly if you yourself are tired. But by following some such routine, you are more likely to end up with your child in bed and asleep than if you just attacked the bedtime problem hit or miss or head on.

Two likes sameness. He likes repetition. And any change is very hard for him. So, as far as you can, permit his toys and other possessions to stay where he puts them, furniture to remain where he expects it to be. He wants everything in its proper place, not only in what he considers its proper place but also at its proper time, each activity of the day following in its customary and predictable order. He likes to know how things will be.

Accept and even welcome the security measures your child sets up for himself, such as his favorite toy or blanket or hat, or even his own thumb. They may be lifesavers.

Even as earlier, take care of the child's lack of inhibition (it is still hard for him not to grab at forbidden objects) with what we have described elsewhere as household engineering. Keep him away from fragile or dangerous objects, or keep them away from him.

Give face-saving commands as much as possible. Try not to trap yourself in some inflexible demand, such as "You have to pick up all your toys before you can have lunch." Far better to suggest, "Let's pick up the toys now." Then if he absolutely refuses to take part in the pickup, you will not be stuck with trying to push through an order in which you may have lost all interest before the situation is terminated.

Good face-saving techniques include:

Say, "Let's do so and so" and then, if need be, you can do the major part of the work yourself.

"How about doing so and so?" is also good. If his answer is "No," so be it. You can give up on the whole thing without embarrassment.

"We'll go and play just as soon as we have picked up."

"Where do the blocks go?"—when it is pickup time—

may motivate the child to put them where they belong. If he doesn't, no matter.

A good face-saving technique, after a child may have refused, is to change the subject or leave the scene completely.

For best results, bypass the rigidities of Two-and-a-half whenever you can. Try to avoid head-on clashes as to whether he will or will not do what you want him to. Chances are that he will not, and if you insist on meeting resistance head-on, you are apt to be the loser. Instead, divert him when you can from what is going on.

If, for example, your child doesn't like to get dressed, try to avoid big arguments about whether he will or will not allow you to put his clothes on him. Instead, set him up on some rather high place and dress him quickly, all the while talking rapidly about some future happening.

It is often possible to divert a child of this age simply with conversation. A good deal of talk tends to confuse the Eighteen-monther, but a rapid chatter, even though he may not entirely understand what you are saying, often serves to interest and even fascinate the Two-and-a-half-year-old. At least it may distract him from whatever position he has taken that is making difficulty.

Avoid the dangerous word "later." Try to avoid giving the child of this age a peg on which to hang his opposition. If, for instance, he wants to do something that will not be appropriate until later, avoid that special word. It will merely activate his own "No," and you may find yourself engaged in a tiresome and fruitless game of "Later," "No, now," "Later," "No, now." Instead, if it must be later, say something like, "OK, we'll do that, but first let's do this or that." You elaborate cheerfully and positively as if you were giving in until (hopefully) he has entirely forgotten his original demand. Or at least you may have stalled him along until actually it is later.

If a request cannot be granted, distraction of any kind may be your best bet and is highly preferable to fighting things out with his own weapons. So, distract, or even better, terminate by changing the scene. If you find yourself involved in one of those fruitless (and boring) "I want—I don't want" routines, in which the child demands some toy, food, article of clothing, or activity, and then the minute he gets it rejects it, and then when you take it away wants it again, it may be impossible to resolve the situation at his level. You will need to break into the impasse. This is best done by shifting to entirely different ground. You can do this by leaving the scene, taking him away from the scene, or introducing some entirely new object or idea.

"I love cookies."

Distracting and terminating may be two of your very best techniques when your child is Two-and-a-half. His best technique is to trap you in his own frustrated back-and-forthness. Whatever the situation, the child of this age tends to want the opposite extreme of whatever you want him to do, or even of what he himself has chosen. You have to help him break into his own back-and-forthness. You almost have to explode him out of his rigidity. This can, of course, be done by your bursting into tears and saying, "You don't love Mommy." It can be done by spanking him or shouting at him. Far better just to distract and change the subject or the scene, if you can.

Since choices are so very hard at this age, it sometimes helps if you can program the child by telling him in advance just what is going to happen. Thus you say, "We're going to the store. You are going to ask the man for chocolate cookies. He is going to put them in a bag for you to carry. Then we're coming home. You may eat one on the way and you will save the rest." His repetition of the sequence of events will show that he at least understands what you are saying and may carry it through.

What about those terrible tantrums, which of course also occurred earlier? Most parents find that their best bet, once a tantrum has begun, is to ignore it as much as they reasonably can. A young child's tantrum can become a powerful weapon if he finds that his parents will do almost anything he wants once he throws a tantrum, so it is very important that he find out as soon as possible that his tantrums are not going to gain him anything, even attention.

But of course your very best technique as far as tantrums are concerned is to prevent them before they begin, if you possibly can. Most parents know what times of the day or what kinds of situations are more than their youngster can stand. At least half the trick, where tantrums are concerned, is to try to keep your child out of the kinds of situations that are going to be just too much for him.

Giving chances is a technique that works very well with some children at some ages. Some even at this tender age respond well to this kind of handling, though some will be too young for it to work.

Questions, if adroitly asked, make excellent motivators at this age. As a question, "Where does your coat go?" is apt to gain a much more positive response than the command, "Hang up your coat." However, be sure to avoid questions that can be answered by "No," such as "Do you want to go now?"

One of the potentially most useful, and at the same time potentially most dangerous, of all techniques at this age is the giving of choices. Used wisely, the giving of choices can get you through many a tense moment, through many a difficult day. Used unwisely, they compound your difficulties. Your very best and chief use of choices at this age comes in situations where the child is stuck and can't move forward, but in which his compliance, at least his compliance in some certain way, is not essential. That is, giving choices can be an excellent motivator if it really doesn't matter too much which alternative is chosen.

Frequently, you can end dawdling and delay, can get your child out of his stuck patterns, by giving some simple choice, such as, "All right now, do you want the blue one or the red one?" Or, "Shall we wash your hands before or after we listen to your record?" Or, "Do you want me to read the book about shoes or the book about squirrels?"

(Especially at Two-and-a-half, the child will usually choose the second alternative simply because it was mentioned last. So, if you yourself do have a preference, it's wise to mention your preferred choice last.)

The feeling that he, himself, is making the choice, that he is doing what he wants rather than what you want, can at times be so marvelously effective that parents sometimes fall into the trap of over-using choices and of using them in certain situations, or with certain children, where they will not be effective and may actually be obstructive. Especially when children are tired, it is important to simplify the situation, not to complicate it by allowing them to make their own choices. Nor is it wise to give choices in really important situations where it seems necessary to you that the child act in a certain way.

Also, personalities differ with respect to choices. There are many children of such a clear-cut temperament that they know their own mind and find it easy to make a choice and stick to it. There are other children who by temperament seem almost constitutionally unable to make a choice. For instance, there are the confused children who do not seem to have any idea of what they want. If you give them a choice, you merely confuse them more.

There is another type of child with whom the use of choices doesn't work very well. This is the kind of child with whom no techniques seem to work. If you give them any possible loophole, such children will start vacillating. If they are given any leeway at all, a simple trip to Grandmother's can be complicated by questions of whether they will or will not go, what they will wear, whether they will sit in the front seat or the back seat of the car, who will sit beside them, and so on and on. For such children, the only effective approach is to tell them specifically and rigidly just exactly what is going to be done, and to insist that your orders be carried out.

Here Are Some Things to Avoid at This Age:

1. Avoid any expectation that all daily routines will go smoothly. Even if you do your best, your child will not always cooperate.

2. Do not introduce any sudden changes in routine without warning or without some cushioning build-up.

3. Avoid any questions that can be answered by "No," such as, "Do you want to have your bath now?"

4. Do not give choices when it matters.

5. Do not expect your child to wait for things or to take turns easily.

6. Try to avoid ultimatums, such as, "You have to eat all your lunch before you can go out and play."

7. Avoid getting all upset by your child's demands and rigidities. Try to see these behaviors not as badness or rebellion, but rather as immaturity. Try to appreciate the wonder and complexity of growing behavior, even when it makes trouble for you.

8. Do not be surprised or upset by "No," or "No, I won't."

9. Do not take away or object to your child's security blanket or favorite, bedraggled toy. Do not fuss at him when he sucks his thumb.

10. Do not expect your child to share easily with other children.

11. Do not be surprised if you are unduly fatigued by the end of the day.

12. Even if your boy or girl behaves exactly in the manner we describe in this book, avoid merely sitting back and telling yourself that he is just going through a stage. He will be going through a stage, but that doesn't mean that you simply sit back and wait for the next stage. You treat him, discipline him, help him, punish him if you must, in your own best way. It is just that knowing that certain undesirable behaviors may be just stages gives you reassurance that other children, too, behave like this; that even bad behaviors can be normal, and that this, too, will pass.

13. Don't worry about your child's IQ (intelligence quotient). There's nothing we know of that you can do that will actually give him a superior mind if the genes you have handed on did not already arrange for that.

14. Refuse to get mixed up in your child's "Mommy do," "Daddy do" routine, which may be very strong, especially at Two-and-a-half. If it is perfectly convenient, allow the person he prefers to take over. But if substitution is not convenient, you keep on helping, whether he prefers you or not.

15. Don't get your feelings hurt if you try to help your child and he wants somebody else. This is just his contrary way and does not mean that he doesn't like you.

Three Years

As at every age, the very best techniques you can use to help your child behave as you wish are those tailored to fit the strong points, and the weak ones, of the age itself. Thus, the more you know about any age — especially the more difficult ones — the more effectively you can fashion your own techniques to match both the age and also the special personality of your own individual child.

When your child is Three, hopefully, you will not be in need of too very many techniques. Life tends to flow quite smoothly for the usual child of this age, and normal parental enthusiasm, stamina, goodwill, ingenuity, and common sense may be all that are needed.

Not so at Three-and-a-half. The child of this age tends to be very hard to handle. It is important to keep in mind, at a time like this, that your child is not your enemy. Those times when a child is at his worst are often the times when he needs the most help from you.

What can you do to help things go smoothly for both of you?

First of all, accept the fact that at this age the child's big emotional struggle is with his mother. She is the one who matters supremely to him. She is the one he needs to conquer. Almost any young child is at his best but also at his worst with his own mother. Never more so than now.

Recognizing this fact, you will if at all possible enlist the services of a good baby-sitter for as much of the time as possible. As we've said before, it may be somewhat deflating to see an untrained high school girl lead your son or daughter smoothly through routines that you, the mother, cannot manage. Why? Because the sitter really does not care deeply if your child fails to dress properly or go to bed quickly. The Three-and-a-half-year old fights only with a worthy opponent—his mother.

This advice may seem like the all-time copout. It remains our best advice.

And once you are away from your son or daughter, try to stay away. If the sitter has him or her out in the yard for the morning, do not keep appearing. If you have managed to get your child down for a nap, do not appear at the door (or window). The mere sight of you may start up unnecessary problems.

Because the child of this age can be so difficult with his mother, we strongly recommend nursery school or at least part time in a day care center. This kind of relief, even three mornings a week, provides a wonderful respite for Mother. Somehow it seems to break into the child's tangled patterns of over-demanding.

Next, we recommend that you enjoy to their fullest those moments between routines when your child may be fun to be with. Enjoy your play with him since he will, if permitted, very much enjoy his play with you.

In fact, your very best technique, at this age or any other, consists, if you can manage it, of establishing a good relationship between the two of you. Your child will at times do many things you want him to just because you are you. So, let him know you care. Let him know you think he or she is just great — the best child ever.

Spend time with him and talk to him. Even at the relatively tender age of Three, your child will enjoy talking to you. The conversation may not be as fully fascinating as it may be when he is older and you really want to know what is on his mind. But if you look forward to the prospect of good conversations later on, now is the time to start.

If your child is one who all of a sudden becomes quite unmanageable in stores or out on a visit, keep such occasions to a minimum. Four will love and will profit from excursions with you. Three-and-a-half may be better off at home.

Remember that the television can be your friend. Wisely used, it can keep a child happy, well behaved and out of difficulty.

If mealtimes are too difficult, and no baby-sitter is at hand, you may find it easiest to provide as best you can and then tell your child, "There it is," and leave the room. Otherwise, every bite may become a bone of contention.

Serious fights over dressing can be diminished by letting the child keep on his T-shirt overnight, and providing pajamas that button in the back. So, instead of having to get two garments off and on, night and morning, there will be few or no over-the-head problems. It will also help if, as you dress him, you can keep his mind off the fact that he is being dressed by talking about some future happy event.

Since emotions at this age tend to be rather fragile, a boy or girl may express many fears, especially fears of people of unusual appearance, of the dark, of animals. Within reason it is best to protect him, or at least support him when he is fearful. Do not be ruled by his fears, but do not, when they are at their height, force him to face the things he fears.

Since the Three-and-a-half-year-old's fears, timidities, and anxieties obviously cause him great concern, try to make him feel comfortable about the things he fears or cannot do. If, briefly, he fears to go outdoors alone, go out with him. If he is afraid of heights or afraid to go down the stairs alone, hold his hand. Or, make up little songs about the things he has trouble with — songs of a positive nature — and sing them to him in a friendly way. When he knows he is not alone with his insecurities and his inadequacies, he will feel a whole lot better.

Four will be a stronger, more secure age. Use this fact in your talks with him. Help him to believe that when he is Four all these things that bother him (you can name each thing specifically) will no longer bother him any more.

From Thirty months on into Three, many children, reverting briefly to babyhood, express a strong need to be carried when out on a walk. Knowing this, the wise mother or sitter will not undertake a walk without some means of homeward transportation — a stroller, wagon, or some other vehicle.

By Three-and-a-half, your walk problems may be different. The child may suddenly stop stock-still and refuse to budge. If walks give too much difficulty, your best bet may be to stay at home for a while and build up new interests inside the house, especially in the kitchen.

Fine motor coordination may now show a tremor. If your child's tremor and lack of coordination cause him difficulty, simply step in without comment and give the support and help he needs. Do not urge him to try harder or to hold his hand steadier. He is already doing the best he can.

If you are one whose child does enjoy an imaginary companion, you can sometimes encourage him to do things nicely in order to set a good example for his companion. If he is one who pretends he is a kitten or a dog, you may find that Kitten will quite willingly and graciously do things that your son, John, habitually refuses. (But in this case you must remember that a kitten has a paw or a chicken a wing. If you want your child to respond to your requests—as in his bath—you had best say, "Come on now, give me your paw," or "How about lifting your wing?")

As at Three, you will, if wise, continue to use face-saving techniques. It is not essential at this time to prove that you are the child's master. It is more important that you and he or she get through the day in one piece, with nerves not too badly frazzled.

So, make heavy use of "How about—", "Let's—", "Maybe you could— ". Use any phrase or any technique that will permit you and/or your child to withdraw gracefully from a situation in which he finds himself unable to comply with your command.

Remember to speak positively rather than negatively. Thus say, "Let's put the books on the shelf," rather than, "Don't throw the books on the floor."

And absolutely refuse to let yourself get mixed up in the preschooler's favorite game of "I don't love you." Just refuse to become emotionally tyrannized by his expressions of affection or disaffection. In his need to control his parent, the child of this age will use emotional threats if they work. See to it they don't.

Distraction, as earlier, is often your best bet with the sticky, stubborn child of this age. If you approach any situation head-on, you are likely to become locked in a life-and-death struggle. Distraction can resolve the issue before the battle is fully joined. So, if you see resistance setting in, talk about something else. Ask your child questions. Pay him a compliment. Tell him something interesting.

Or, make a sudden noise. Just clapping your hands together may do the trick. Or, turn on some music. Or, show him something attractive. Or, if things look really bad, produce a bit of his favorite food.

In thinking about techniques, it is important to keep in mind that some are virtually foolproof and will work with almost any child at almost any time. Others depend a great deal on timing, or on the child's age and individuality. Thus, most parents discover rather early whether their child is one who is helped and protected by an advance warning, or if he is one on whom you do best to spring things.

This brings up the question of whether, if you are going out in the evening, you should give advance warning and/or say a formal goodbye. Or if you should just sneak out, dishonest as this may seem. Only a trial-and-error will tell you what works best with your own special child.

Actually, neither may work. Three-and-a-half-year-olds, along with their other fears, may express an almost hysterical fear of having their parents go out in the evening. Though no parent likes to be controlled by a child's demands, right while this special fear is at its height it may be kinder to keep evening absences at a minimum. This kind of anxiety, fortunately, is usually not long-lived.

Things to Avoid:

1. Try to avoid the feeling that your child should or ought always to behave nicely, or that routines should always go smoothly if only you do the right thing. Especially at Three-and-a-half, there may normally be much daily conflict.

2. Don't feel guilty, or that you are passing the buck, if you leave a substantial amount of your child's care to a sitter, since many at this age do best with someone other than their own mother.

3. Even at this (relatively) late age, do not be unhappy if your child still sucks his thumb or cuddles his security blanket.

4. Do not conclude, just because your child may suddenly stumble and stutter, tremble and twitch, that something is necessarily wrong with him. Many boys and girls quite normally express great motor uncertainty, especially at Three-and-a-half.

5. Don't worry if your Three-year-old no longer sleeps at nap time. A mere play nap may give perfectly adequate relief to both mother and child.

Avoid correcting your child's speech, though if he puts ¡gether incorrectly, you can repeat it, using the correct ɔid trying too hard to help him get over stuttering or any infantile articulation. Enjoy each stage of his language growth, no matter how immature.

7. Try to avoid feeling that your child is not eating as much as he should. Chances are that his own appetite may be his best guide as to how much to eat.

8. Don't feel that you have a bed-wetting problem if your child still wets the bed at night, some nights or even every night. Many quite normal children do not develop the ability to stay dry until they are Five or even Six years of age. (Pad them up good and tight to save on laundry, and don't make a fuss.)

9. Do not feel that you should be teaching your child to read. Read to him all you can. Make books available. Let him see that you enjoy reading. But don't try to teach him to read for himself.

Four Years

The techniques with which one can best handle the bouncy Four-year-old stem directly from a knowledge of his basic personality. Obviously, the better you understand him, the better job you will do in helping him behave in ways that will please you rather than grieve you.

To begin with, Four is one who loves adventures. Share them with him. Create them for him. A simple trip around your own neighborhood, with its inevitable points of interest, takes on new luster when seen through the enthusiastic eyes of a Four-year-old. And when you plan an excursion, plan it with him in mind. A short walk, perhaps past a spot where a new building is going up (or better still, being torn down), and an ice-cream cone on the way back will be a lot more satisfactory to a Four-year-old than a cultural expedition to a nearby town.

The best way to calm Four down when some of his wilder ways (his profanity, his boasting, his super-silly way of talking)

bother you is to ignore him. An opposite technique, and one that is perhaps equally effective, is to join in and enjoy. You will not enjoy his profanity, but you can often enjoy his exaggerated stories by countering with your own — obvious — exaggeration. That is, rein in when you feel that you absolutely need to, but do not always rein in.

Certainly, you can join in with and truly enjoy some of the wonderfully silly poems and stories now available for the Four-year-old. You haven't lived if you have never shared with a Four-year-old the delightful nonsense of a book such as Ruth Kraus' *I Want to Paint My Bathroom Blue*, which tells you of

"A doorknob a doorknob, a deer little doorknob,
A deerknob a deerknob, a door little deerknob."

To be certain that you take the time for the excursions and adventures that the Four-year-old so loves, you may like to set aside one afternoon a week, or part of an afternoon, that will be **his**. He may choose (from a list prepared by you to be sure that things don't get too wild) the destination or activity that will please him for that particular week. He or she may even like to keep a little notebook, with considerable help from you, of course, that tells about these weekly excursions.

Since the child of this age does tend to go out-of-bounds, you will need, for safety, to find the most effective way of contain-

47

ing him within what you consider to be acceptable physical limits. Environmental restrictions such as gates or closed doors are not as effective as earlier, but most at this age do respond pretty well to verbal restrictions, such as "as far as the corner." In fact, that Four-year-old seems to like and respect boundaries and limits, which he doesn't have within himself. He seems to appreciate it when you supply them.

Most respond rather well to the statement, "It's the rule that..." even when they do not understand why it is the rule.

With some boys and girls, a very good technique at this age is bargaining. If it bothers you to do this, or if it seems too much like bribing, don't do it. But with Fours, many parents find that a little bargaining goes a long way. That is, you give a little, and your child may be willing and able to give a little in return.

Since this is an age when children love tricks and new ways of doing things, sometimes if a child balks or stalls you can motivate him by suggesting that he hop or skip toward some desired destination.

Although positive instructions tend to work better than negative — that is, tell him what you want him to do, not what you do not want him to do — the negative can at times be used effectively. An exaggeration of the negative such as "Never, never, never!", if expressed forcefully, may engage his attention and his compliance. It's best in general, however, to keep things positive if you can. If you tell a child how nicely he is going to behave, he sometimes does so.

As just earlier, the child tends to respond very well to the notion of newness. Such words as "different," "surprise," "guess what" are still highly effective as motivators, as they were just earlier. Also, as just earlier, whispering may be more effective than shouting. At least it calms the child and catches his attention.

Since Fours love exaggeration, in your efforts to motivate or restrain, as well as in your efforts to entertain, you will find exaggeration to be very effective. "As big as the world," "in ten million years," or just plain silly language such as "mitsy, bitsy, witsy," "goofy, woofy, spoofy," can often interest or distract when distraction is needed, as it so often will be.

At Four, perhaps even more than at other ages, praise and compliments work wonders. Later on, children may be aware of exaggeration, but no compliment seems too much for Four's insatiable appetite. In fact, if you don't praise enough, he will praise himself: "I'm smart."

At this or any other age, the simple act of conversing with your child can work wonders. Almost any child loves to feel that he has his parents full attention, and he loves to talk. If you want to know what is on your child's mind, you don't necessarily need to ask directly. Just talk with him. Good communication is vital in those difficult teen years soon to come, but it is important even here. So listen to your child and talk to him. Conversation provides one of the best routes to a good relationship, and in the final analysis it is your relationship with your child, even more than the use of good techniques, that gets you through the day.

There is one aspect of the world today, often criticized and seldom praised, that can nevertheless help you out beautifully, especially on a rainy day. Do take advantage, freely though carefully, of one of the new things society has to offer for the preschooler — television. Don't be afraid, within reason, to take advantage of what your television screen has to offer. It can be one of your best techniques for filling some of the day and for meeting Four's high demand for excitement, activity and drama.

The choice of suitable programs may be difficult, but try to select one program that you consider good for your child that will become his program. Then he can be more easily controlled in not being exposed to other programs that may be both frightening and beyond his comprehension. Television won't teach your child to read, as some programs claim to be able to do. But if you and your child enjoy this kind of program, so be it.

Last of all, remember that once you appreciate what a child of this age (or any age) is like, it helps you to appreciate what he will like. You can tailor your techniques accordingly.

Things to Avoid:

1. Don't worry excessively if your Four-year-old, as he very likely will, goes out-of-bounds. A certain extra exuberance is natural, usual, and quite probably necessary at this age to give balance between uncertain Three-and-a-half and quiet, adaptable Five.

2. Don't fuss too much and certainly don't worry if your boy or girl, lies, swears, and/or exaggerates. Such behaviors are almost the essence of Four-year-oldness. You can, and undoubtedly will, discourage and disapprove of such behaviors, but try not to worry about them.

3. Avoid that wild search for things that will motivate an uninterested or underactive child. Success is the best motivator for any child at any age. The likelihood is that any child will be motivated to activity if you provide for him materials and opportunities that, by his temperament and maturity level, he will be able to cope with and to deal with effectively.

4. Don't worry that you should be doing something to increase you child's intelligence. Basic intelligence is, so far as we know, largely determined by genetic factors. You can and should give all children reasonable stimulation, but don't be self-conscious about level or quality of intelligence.

5. Don't feel that you should be teaching your Four-year-old to read.

6. Don't blame your child's playmates for behaviors in him or her that you don't like—exhibitionism, bad language, sex play and the like. Today it may be a neighboring child who initiates the activity. Tomorrow it may be your own!

7. Don't fail to enjoy this extremely amusing, lively, enthusiastic age while it lasts, even though some aspects of your child's behavior may not be entirely charming.

Five Years

Let us at this point take a deep breath and make the bold assumption that your Five-year-old is behaving in a way which we have found to be characteristic of a typical child of this age who has the good fortune to be growing up in a well adjusted family.

That is, let us assume that he is friendly, loving, appreciative, that he wants to please you and to do the right things, that he wants and means to be good. Chances are that even if he is, you may attribute his good behavior, as you may earlier have attributed any bad behaviors, to something that is happening in the environment. Parents of Two-and-a-half-year-olds, for instance, often attribute the difficult behavior so often seen at this age to the bad example of neighboring children or of the boys and girls met at nursery school or a day care center.

We once knew a pair of parents who attributed their Five-year-old son's good behavior to the fact that the family was spending the year in England, where they felt the discipline was better than in the United States and, therefore, he was exposed to more well behaved contemporaries than he would have been at home.

We don't think that the environment, important as it obviously is, is chiefly responsible for age changes in behavior. And so we genuinely believe that if all goes well, Five-year-olds wherever they live, tend to be gratifyingly well behaved, and that it is easy and natural for most of them, most of the time, to behave nicely. And to be rather easy to discipline.

Thus we shall go very lightly in giving advice about Fives, stressing instead, in the next section, that time when your child will be approaching, and experiencing, Six.

Certainly, good as Five may be, much of the time, any Five-year-old, like the child of any age, will have bad moments, even bad days. Otherwise he would not be normal. When he is naughty, as he will be sometimes, you may indeed need to resort to punishment. (The optimistic things we say in this book about the wonderful effects one may expect from understanding your child, do not imply that difficulties will not arise. And though we do not define discipline as punishment and do not equate the two, at any age, even this best of ages, you will and must expect to do some punishing. (We refer you to our chapter on Punishment, which applies even at this usually favorable age.)

However, best of all in the line of disciplining is knowing a lot about what is and is not reasonable to expect of a Five-year-old. Many things parents consider as bad and thus punishable are often simply immaturities. That is, sometimes we expect too much of the child and then punish because he fails to meet our excessive expectations. In a way, this is what this book is all about.

Here are a few special areas in which parents sometimes expect too much. The ordinary Five-year-old does not find it easy to admit wrongdoing. So, if for instance, you ask him if he was the one who broke the vase (and you are very sure he did), chances are he will say he didn't.

If all evidence suggests that he is the culprit, try asking him how he broke it. Often his review of what happened can be very touching: "Well, I was going round the corner of the table too fast and I didn't see the vase."

If you feel you must punish for the vase breaking (though it would have been better in the first place to have the vase out of reach), do so. But do not, in addition, punish your child for lying about whether or not he did it.

Actually, even in less hazardous situations, the ordinary Five-year-old is by no means always truthful. He tries to tell the truth but is not always successful.

Nor can Five always resist taking things that belong to other people. His wants tend to be rather strong and his sense of other people's property rather weak. Certainly, taking things should not be condoned. But parents should not be surprised if it occurs. The child will need to be quite a bit older before his appreciation of other people's property rights equals his appreciation of his own. (Some Fives show they know they have done wrong by hiding or destroying a stolen object.)

At any rate, prevention is infinitely better than punishment. If you must punish, do so as calmly as possible. Fortunately, at Five, the child's wish to be good and to do the right thing is strong. With luck, much of the time — at least till Five-and-a-half moves on toward Six — there should be relatively little need for punishment.

Six Years

There is probably no age other than Six at which the use of techniques is more greatly needed or more rewardingly effective. We cannot absolutely **guarantee** their effectiveness, but your chances are excellent that they will work. In fact, it is often little less than miraculous to see a raging tyrant turn into a friendly companion just because you have managed to say the right thing.

Technique Number One — **Praise**. It may not be easy to find something you can praise, but at least try.

Next, and another of our favorites, is **Chances**. Many a Six-year-old may meet almost any direct command with "No, I won't." Ignoring this obvious refusal, and refusing to meet resistance head-on, try saying, "I guess you're going to need three chances on that one." Clearly relieved that he could resist so blatantly, and still have half a chance to avoid open battle, the usual Six-year-old will use up all but his last chance, and then comply with your original request.

Counting works almost as well as chances. You ask your boy or girl to do some simple thing. He or she just stands there. So you say, calmly and confidently, "And let's see if you can do it before I count to ten." (Or whatever.) This gives your child time to pull himself (or herself) together. And allows you to slow down on your counting in case compliance is lagging.

Or, similarly, you can use time marks on the clock: "When the big hand is at the top, it will be time to pick up your toys." That is, your child does not have to comply at once, but you have given warning that compliance will eventually be expected.

Technique Number Four is to **Sidestep** the issue. Don't meet violence with violence. Instead of meeting defiance head-on, just change the subject or situation. Many Sixes use up what defiance they have in their initial "No, I won't," or "Try and make me." They may be as relieved as you that war does not have to develop.

One help to you in sidestepping or dodging the issue is to give as few direct commands as possible. This you will have found useful at earlier ages. And as late as Six, unless a direct command actually needs to be made, you will save time and trouble by giving your orders obliquely.

Technique Number Five is simple—just **Bargain**. You shouldn't depend on this in every situation. It is not only time-consuming but may give the impression of weakness on your part. But at times it works nicely. One little girl we know loved popsicles. Her mother bargained with her that if she would try very hard not to fight with her brother so much, she could have a popsicle every day.

Technique Number Six may indeed seem like weakness to some of you, but it is often highly successful and can provide a wonderfully welcome relief to an embattled mother and child. **Give in**. Sometimes you find yourself giving orders and commands or making rules about things that really don't matter. So if something you have asked your child to do is greatly resisted, you could pause a moment, think it over and say, "Well, OK, I guess it really doesn't make all that much difference."

These are our very best techniques, but there are, of course, many other things you can try which are in general use. **Isolation**, or removing the child from the scene, or just temporarily separating the two of you from each other, can be effective.

Perhaps one of the most customary techniques used by parents of Six-year-olds is **Ignoring**. As at the earlier but similarly difficult age of Two-and-a-half, many parents find that they do best not to notice every naughty thing their child does. Some really dangerous behaviors, of course, must be checked. But there are other things you really don't like which probably do not actually do major harm. If and when you can comfortably do so, ignore them. Since punishment, though often deserved, does not do much to improve behavior at Six, perhaps the less of it the better.

Experienced parents are usually quite aware of the kinds of situations which bring on their own child's worst behavior. This awareness can help avoid times, places, and arrangements of people which are most certain to bring on disaster. For instance, having guests in your household tends to bring on a Six-year-old's very worst behavior—loud, silly showing off and a total deafness to your commands and suggestions.

Techniques suggested for guests in the home of the typical Six-year-old include: (1) Bring him a present. (2) Let him have a turn showing off by bouncing his ball or standing on his head or doing his other tricks. (3) Then you—or some other adult— let him take you to his room for a while to show you his toys, leaving the other guests in peace.

Best to do this early, while he is still on his relatively good behavior, rather than to let things go too far and then have to take him out of the room as a punishment.

Since Six seems not always able to tell the difference between mine and thine, he often steals. Usually this is restricted to taking small sums of money or objects from his parents' bureaus or desks. The best technique in such instances, aside from the usual explanations about not taking things that belong to others, is to lock up desk and bureau drawers. Tell the child you are doing this to help him remember.

Fortunately, in many boys and girls, behavior tends to quiet down around Six-and-a-half or Seven. But between Five-and-a-half and Six-and-a-half, most parents find they need to use all the techniques they can think of.

Seven Years

The basic message of this book is that the most effective discipline is that which is built around the characteristics and nature of the child being disciplined. We know that the typical Seven-year-old is a procrastinator with a very short memory and a tendency to get distracted.

Taking these three traits into consideration, a parent may approach discipline in the following way. Suppose your child is watching television and you want him to take out the trash. Clearly he will not relish leaving his program to carry out this uninteresting task. (In fact, whatever they may be doing, most Sevens are not much interested in helping around the house.) You warn him in advance: "Just as soon as your program is over, I'd like you to take out the wastebaskets."

But — you can count on it — he will forget your request long before his program is over. So you remind him, "Now that your program is over, how about the trash?" Most, though not all, will comply fairly willingly. Only one last hazard. The child is likely to get sidetracked along the way. Step three is to check to see that this doesn't happen.

It may seem easier to do the work yourself. But most of us feel that some responsibility around the house is good for the child, and this is the way we recommend that a parent go about it. In fact, whatever the situation or circumstance, Seven needs quite a lot of reminding, and one of the frequently voiced complaints of the child of this age is, "But you didn't remind me!" Six may want and need three chances to do things right. Eight may want only an oblique comment or hint. But Seven likes to be warned ahead of time and then reminded, and does best with rather specific instructions.

Though even grown-ups are not entirely immune to the use of special techniques, your typical Seven-year-old is not as vulnerable or responsive to them as he was only a year earlier. Many of your best techniques will simply be ignored. Or the child may turn the tables on you. Six, stubborn and oppositional, will often fall for the simple command, "Before I count to ten, I want you to start cleaning up your room." Seven may take over this technique and tell you, "Before I count to ten, I want to see a glass of juice on this table."

Thus, many parents find that in place of techniques, they get the best results if they can establish and maintain a good, responsive relationship with their Sevens. One of the most widely recommended ways of doing this is the so-called feedback method. According to this method, your son comes home from school and tells you that all the kids hate him and are mean to him. You merely repeat to him what he has said: "Oh, you feel that all the kids hate you and are mean to you."

This rather simple feedback supposedly lets the child know that you are listening to him and that you understand and sympathize with what he is saying. It has two disadvantages. One is that sometimes it makes the child angry: "That's what I just said!" he will tell you. The other is that it is not particularly constructive. Although it shows that you are listening and presumably that you are sympathetic, it does not lead to positive action.

Even sometimes gloomy Seven can be moved to more constructive action or attitude if you handle feedback a little more creatively. You might try, "It seems to you that the kids don't like you and are mean to you. What happened?" It may then turn out that some child called him a name. ("Retard" and "gay" are among the more popular epithets.) You can then, we hope, work out with him what is the best thing to do when called names.

Sympathetic discussion is nearly always helpful. But it is best to guard against being too sympathetic, and agreeing with the child that the teacher is an old meanie and the other kids a pretty rotten bunch. As Haim Ginott, probably the first psychologist to recommend feedback has emphasized, you don't deny your child's perceptions. You accept them as the way things seem to him, but then you try to head him toward more positive perceptions.

Thus, when your child complains, "You always make me do all the work around here," when some very simple household task is required, a response such as "Oh, it seems to you that you have to do all the work around here. How can we schedule things to make them fairer?" may get you further than outright denial, a lecture on responsibilities, or a long story about how when you were young you not only walked five miles to school through the snow but did practically all the housework single-handed.

Fortunately, when things go wrong, Seven is more capable of recovery than he was at Six. Now the child can often pull himself together enough to be able to plan how the problem could be solved should a similar situation arise in the future.

Praise, though most children like it, seems somewhat less successful as a motivator at this age than at Six, or at Eight. Sometimes you can get a child to do what you want by reminding him of how things seem to other people. There is a certain awareness of others that was definitely missing at Six.

Discipline, as we have emphasized, is not just a matter of punishing for wrongdoing. Discipline ideally involves helping a child to behave in such a way that eventually he will grow to be a self-disciplined, effective, mature adult.

Seven, when given a direction or command, is less likely than Six to refuse outright. Instead of "No, I won't," or "Try and make me," your child is more apt to ask, "Why do I have to?" "Because I say so" may often turn out to be an adequate answer, since Seven is usually asking not so much to find out the reason as simply to stall. However, if you feel that he really wants to know, tell him.

Now and then, giving in on your part can work wonders. Suppose you've given a routine command to "Be sure to wear your sweater, rubbers, mittens" and the child comes back with "Why do I have to?" Maybe it really isn't necessary. Perhaps you could, on occasion say, "Oh, well, maybe you don't need to."

For any communication or request to be effective, of course, the child needs first to hear what you say. Often he or she really does not hear. Many parents of Sevens suspect deafness since the child can, at times, look right at you and seem not to hear what you say. More likely, it is not deafness but mere inattention. Seven lives so deeply within himself that much of the time he tunes out the outside world. So before you assume that the child has heard you, it may be wise to make sure that this is the case. "Did you hear what I said?" will often reveal that he didn't.

Make your rules—for instance that there is to be no hitting—and then when hitting occurs, take whatever disciplinary action you have planned and promised, at once. Do not make the same threats over and over again and then not carry them out. Threats about what you will do the very next time something happens, especially if customarily not carried out, tend to fall on deaf ears.

Eight Years

Perhaps the most important factor in the discipline of the Eight-year-old is his strong, emotional tie to his mother. Ever alert not only to what she does and says but also to what he believes she thinks and feels, Eight is strongly influenced by her wishes and desires. He will go out of his way to do things he doesn't really want to do simply to please his mother.

If Mother can keep the relationship smooth, can manage to put in the extra time, care, attention, sensitivity needed, she really has an ace up her sleeve. Often a mere look from mother—something which in a few short years will have virtually no effect—can at this tender age stop bad behavior short, and encourage good and compliant behavior.

Leaning on his hope for special intimacy between himself and his mother, a boy may ask her, tentatively, "Instead of calling me to come to dinner, could you just say 'Wahoo wahoo' and I'll know what you mean?" A girl may request, "Instead of telling me to wash my hands to get ready for lunch, could you just say 'Hands?'" It is, of course, sensible to give in to such demands.

Along these same lines, you can make similar suggestions yourself, planning that when you say certain things — perhaps some special code word — he or she will respond in some certain way.

Time alone with Mother tends to be so much treasured that, in this respect, you can often bargain a little. If your son or daughter will do certain things, behave in certain ways, it will then work out that the two of you will have time to do some desirable thing together.

A certain alertness on your part is needed here. But since so many things that the child of this age does are done in order to win your approval, it is important to keep an eye out for them, and to be lavish with your praise and expressions of approval.

The child's incessant demand for Mother's time, attention and appreciation can indeed be a bit draining. But it definitely has its good side — ensures that you, the parent, have something your child wants and cares about (your time, attention, affection) and which he will go out of his way to win.

He wants your approval, wants to please and satisfy. You, the parent, can be more successful in your discipline if your demands and expectations are reasonable, if they fit with what your boy or girl can actually perform. A major key as to how much general goodness and cooperation one can reasonably expect is found in the level of his ethical sense. Thus, a typical Four-year-old tends to have little respect for telling the truth; may in fact lie like a trooper. Eight, though a long way from perfection in this respect, much of the time can be counted on to tell the truth about things that matter.

We summarize major highlights in the ethical sense of the typical Eight-year-old as follows:

For all his expansiveness and exaggeration, the child of Eight is basically a rather reasonable person. On many occasions, parents find that he can listen to reason and even can change his mind if he can be convinced that his own position is unreasonable. He can also make up his mind more easily than he could when younger.

Eights as a rule have a fairly clear idea of goodness and badness, right and wrong. The child is beginning to think more abstractly. Good and bad are no longer simply things that parents permit or forbid. Eight wants and means to be good, and tries hard to live up to his own standards and to what he thinks are the adults' standards.

Most Eight-year-olds are fairly good about taking the blame if they have done wrong. They may excuse their misdeed with "Do you blame me?", "Could I help it?", or may deny their guilt, but not blame somebody else as they might have done earlier.

Truthfulness may not be the Eight-year-old's strong point. His natural expansiveness tends to lead to boasting, exaggeration and even the telling of tall tales. However, Eights can usually distinguish fact from fantasy and can usually be counted on to tell the truth about important matters.

Eight-year-olds tend to be extremely interested in and concerned about their own possessions. They like to acquire and barter objects, like to arrange them, gloat over them. Not the least of their property interest is in money. Their love of money unfortunately sometimes leads them to take household money, in order to treat their friends. However, many are interested enough in money to be willing to work for it. Money can sometimes be a good motivator.

Thus, it's fair to say that the typical Eight-year-old is, in general, moving toward a reasonably good ethical sense though in some respects, admittedly, he still has rather a long way to go, and certain lapses must be expected and allowed for.

Nine Years

Admittedly, all good things must one day come to an end. And so it is with the concept of techniques. For the first six or seven years of your child's life they do work, often like magic. But even by Seven or Eight, and definitely by Nine, these wonderful helpers for getting your girl or boy to behave as you wish lose their charm and effectiveness.

Certainly, even adults, at times, use some sort of techniques with each other. The mother who says to her children, "Wait till after your father has had his dinner before you ask him," is using a technique. Anyone who approaches another person tactfully or who uses his knowledge of the other person's personality to obtain a desired result is in a way using a technique.

But techniques as little tricks, or specific and special ways of approaching another person in order to gain his or her compliance, are no longer particularly useful with your Nine-year-old girl or boy.

However, since much discipline involves the child's ability to distinguish good from bad, right from wrong, truth from untruth, it can be useful at Nine as at any other age for a parent to know what is reasonable and what is unreasonable to expect of any child with regard to his so-called ethical sense. Here is a brief summary of our own research findings:

Response to Directions, Punishment and Praise: In some children, Nine may be an age of considerable rebellion against authority. Some Nines, however, merely rebel by withdrawing — they can look right through you as you give a command and not hear you. Or they rebel by complaining but actually do carry out your commands. Gradually the complaints, rebellions, and anxieties diminish as the Nine-year-old approaches the usually peaceful age of Ten.

Most at Nine can interrupt their own activity in response to a demand from an adult. Securing the child's attention may depend on his interest and willingness to carry out the request; and like his younger self, Nine may wish to postpone whatever it is until later, and then forget. Thus, Nines still need to be given rather detailed directions, and if they do not comply at once, may need to be reminded. In fact, most Nines are relatively easy to discipline, but do require a good deal of reminding.

In general, there is much less arguing back than earlier. If the child does not like the direction you give, he may look sulky, cross or truculent, but if no issue is made of this, he will usually obey.

Many prefer a reasonable appraisal of their work to praise, though praise is always welcome. And if they do resist, a threat of deprivation of some desired object or activity usually suffices to bring them back into line. Isolation works well with some. They may be "sore" at punishment, calling it "a gyp," "not fair," or "just my hard luck," but most take criticism better than formerly, especially if it is carefully phrased. Nines tend to go to extremes. They may take authority on themselves to invite a friend home to lunch and then ask permission for some very small, unimportant thing.

In response to directions, we have found that Six tends to say, "I won't." Seven says, "Do I have to?" Eight agrees, "If you insist." Nine complies, "All right."

Responsiveness to Reason: Most Nines can make up their minds easily, and some can change an original decision in response to reason, though this does not hold up for all issues.

Sense of Good and Bad: There is now less concern than earlier about good and bad as such. Now most girls and boys seem to think more in terms of right and wrong. They want to do things the right way and may be ashamed of being wrong. Many are able to say they are sorry when they do wrong. There is now great interest in fairness, especially fairness of parents and teachers. Nines are extremely concerned that any punishment they receive be fair. They also want other children to be fair.

Group standards are now more important to most Nines than parental standards, even though they realize that they have to respect the latter. They like to evaluate the behavior of other children: "He's a good (or poor) sport." They tend to be disgusted with others who do not live up to the standards of the group. Most are quite exacting not only of others but of themselves.

Blaming and Alibiing: In keeping with their strong feelings about fairness, children of this age want any blame that may be given to be apportioned fairly. There is much interest in who started any difficulty. They try to explain their own behavior and may try to reason and explain their way out of any difficulty.

Some can accept blame and say, "I did it and I'm sorry." They may even feel ashamed of their own wrong doing, but are very upset if blamed for something they didn't do.

Truth and Honesty: Nines are usually quite truthful about their own misdeeds and lapses from virtue. Discipline is thus made easier, because at least parents do not have to go scurrying around trying to get to the bottom of things.

Though an exuberant Eight, for the most part honest and truthful, does sometimes expand into not entirely truthful exaggeration, or an occasional pilfering of family money to buy things he needs, the Nine-year-old has improved considerably in both respects. He might stray from the truth to protect a friend's lie, but even when he exaggerates, he often sets things right by saying, "Oh, Mom, you know that isn't really true."

Nines rarely take things that don't belong to them, and if they do, they may want to return them to set things right. Most are now developing a real sense of ethical standards and most mean to live up to them.

The words "honesty" and "truth" are now becoming part of the child's own vocabulary. He may say, "I'll have to be honest." Certainly, at least, the rudiments of a conscience are developing.

Ten Years and After

With any luck, your Ten-year-old will be, most of the time, one of the joys of your life. This can be, above all others, a truly golden age in which the child is happy and well adjusted, comfortable with himself and with those about him, especially with his family. Like his earlier Five-year-old self, he wants and means to do things right, to be a good member of his family, and to a large extent, he succeeds. Thus, for many, except for temporary flare-ups, discipline is not a major problem.

After Ten, it's a whole new story. It's a time when the rather simplistic techniques we have been describing by no means do the trick. In these ages, even more so than earlier, it is your relationship with and the extent to which you are able to communicate with your boy or girl that makes the difference. Not even an extremely authoritative book can guarantee success.

The teens, and even the preteens, are above all a time of rebellion, a time of defining one's self as apart from and separate from one's mother and father. Since rebellion is the name of the game, discipline during these years tends to be exceptionally difficult.

Our position with regard to the child of any age is that the more you, the parent, know about the kind of behavior to be expected at that particular age, as well as the more you know about the individuality of your own particular child, the better. Thus, assuming that your own teenager's behavior remains within what one refers to as normal limits, we can offer you information about what in general you can expect at these older ages in our book, *Your Ten- to Fourteen-Year-Old*, by Ames, Ilg, and Baker.

However, especially today, the behavior of many teenagers goes considerably beyond what anyone could describe as normal limits. In some families, in fact in some communities, running away, drug use and teenage pregnancy are not unusual occurrences. For families in which teenage behavior is truly out of bounds, family therapy, assuming that you can persuade your girl or boy to take part, will definitely be in order and has been known to do wonders. Before you resort to this expedient, however, you may well find help in some of the strong and practical books now available. We especially recommend *How to Deal With Your Acting-Up Teenager*, by Bayard and Bayard, or *Toughlove*, by York, York and Wachtel.

The teens aren't easy in the best of families, but most of us do survive them.

TECHNIQUES VARY WITH AGE

How well a discipline technique works depends largely on the age of the child. The following table lists techniques that tend to work at different ages.

DISCIPLINE TECHNIQUES AND AGE CHANGES

18 months: Doesn't easily obey direct commands. Attention must be gotten by doing something child likes and wants to share. Technique: Pick up and put child where wanted.

2 1/2 years: Age of opposite extremes. Techniques: Avoid giving choices. Avoid questions that can be answered by no. Use routines. Talk and work fast so child will be doing what is wanted before she or he has time to think and rebel.

3 1/2 years: Difficulty making changes. May be good in long periods of play, but very poor at changing from one activity to another. Techniques: Simplify changes as much as possible. Avoid head-on clashes. Give in when things aren't important. Change subject or distract by bringing in something nice so child forgets to object. At this age children are much better with almost anyone other than the principal caregiver.

4 years: Out-of-bounds age. Delights in upsetting adults. Techniques: Pretend to ignore wild behavior, if possible. Try to keep child so interested and excited in positive ways that there's no need for out-of-bounds behavior. Make few rules, but enforce these strictly.

5 1/2- 6 years: Age of extreme imbalance. May be very rude, resistant, defiant. Thrives on head-on clashes. Techniques: Try to avoid such clashes, nobody wins. Patience and skill are needed. Ignore refusal or be impersonal when child answers commands with "I won't." Use praise.

7 years: Obedience problem isn't so much defiance as that child is sidetracked. Technique: To have simple chore done, tell child in advance. Be sure the directions have been heard. Remind child before he or she forgets and does something else.

8 years: Easily disappointed if what an adult says or does isn't what the child wants. Technique: Give commands in ways acceptable to the child.

9 years: Interests are beginning to spread beyond home and family. May resist feelings of being a little child and of being told what to do. Technique: Save direct commands for big, important matters.

Household Engineering

In earlier times, as already noted, discipline in many households used to mean punishment. Parents whose discipline was rated good by friends and neighbors were those who made very strict rules about behavior, and severely punished any infringement. Some boys and girls were not entirely sure what **all** the rules were, so they often waited apprehensively to see if they were going to be punished or not. But the responsibility was theirs, and their efforts were directed into **not** doing things that would make their parents, especially their father, angry.

I once knew a family in which, when time came for father to come home from work, the mother would warn, "Now children, don't get your father started." However, somebody was sure to misstep and firm punishment would inevitably follow.

Many parents today take a quite different approach. The burden of proof for them now lies not entirely on the child but at least, in part, on them. Their effort is, to a large extent, directed toward arranging the household and the family living in such a way that, with luck, it is easy for the child to behave in ways which will be comfortable not only for him but for the rest of the family as well.

This concept was once described by Dr. Frances L. ILg, former Director of the Gesell Institute, as household engineering. It applies most appropriately to the rather young child, whose active body and insatiable curiosity lead all too often into difficulty.

Keeping Fragile Objects Out Of Reach

Though there are undoubtedly individuals today who still believe that even very small children should be taught **not to touch** forbidden objects, most of us now recommend keeping such objects out of reach. It is not weakness but rather common sense, if you are the parent of a preschooler, to put breakable vases or candy dishes up on a mantlepiece or high shelf. The effort involved in teaching a Two-to-Four-year-old not to touch such objects is not necessarily worthwhile when it is so easy to make them unavailable. Electric outlets can be covered in such a way as to make them safe from the prying fingers of a toddler. Medicines, obviously, must be kept in very high or preferably locked cabinets. Matches most certainly must be kept out of reach. Standing lamps should have solid bases which make them hard to tip over.

"Can you blame me?"

Keeping The Child Out Of Dangerous Areas

One can keep fragile or breakable objects out of reach and thus unavailable to the child, or one can, conversely, keep the child away from the objects. A gate or two can keep boy or girl out of rooms which may be difficult to child-proof. They are especially useful in households where staircases present an all-too-tempting and all-too-dangerous source of accident. If the child cannot reach the stairs, he cannot fall down them. The kitchen stove can be made unavailable in most households by using a little gate or fence.

For the infant, the often much maligned playpen can be a lifesaver. There are some who feel that a playpen hampers the child's free spirit and is bad for his psyche. We still favor this device. If equipped with interesting toys, and especially if kept in a room in sight of other people, it can provide many happy hours for the baby, who presumably will not be getting into difficulty while so protected. And it can provide many hours of peace and freedom for the baby's mother.

Scheduling Can Help

Disciplinary problems having to do with sibling difficulties can sometimes be solved before they occur simply by dovetailing your children's schedules. Admittedly, if two young children nap at the same time, this provides mother with a free hour or two. But if they nap at different times, this provides two hours or more when they are not available to each other, and may thus be well worth the effort.

A different aspect of scheduling which can prevent much undesirable behavior (for which a parent may then feel called upon to discipline) is to be aware of times of day when a young boy or girl may be especially tired and fractious, and thus inclined to get into difficulty. The hour or so just before dinner tends to be an especially dangerous period. Tired and hungry, your preschooler is all too likely to engage in forbidden, undesirable or even dangerous behaviors. Busy as the adult may be at this time of day, accept the fact that attention from you **before** rather than after the undesirable behavior occurs will prevent the need for disciplinary action. Providing a bit a food, even though you may fear this will spoil the child's appetite, may be the course of wisdom.

Household Engineering Cannot Do Everything

Any parents, knowing their own households, can adapt this general notion of household engineering to their own special needs. The term "child-proofing" is part of today's vocabulary. Child-proofing is not really tremendously difficult to arrange, once you put your mind to it.

But whatever the term you have in mind — household engineering, child-proofing — does not mean that the environment has to do it all. Gradually, as your toddler grows older, certain rules can be established. We know of one very bookish family which obviously could not remove all books from the household or put them out of reach. So they picked out one attractive and flashy book, not on the child's bookshelf but on a shelf with books reserved for adults, and called it "Becky's book." When tired of her own books, this little girl would go unerringly to the grown-up part of the library and pick out "Becky's book."

There is, obviously, much that a parent can and will need to do to maintain good discipline, other than keeping breakable or dangerous objects away from the child, or the child away from breakable or dangerous objects. But even a little thought given to physical arrangements or schedules can prevent many of the more customary disciplinary problems from occurring in the first place.

Children Differ

Though there are many exceptions, most parents and other adults in charge take a remarkably responsible attitude toward child behavior. If things in the household are not harmonious, many parents — especially mothers — blame themselves. Many of us have in our minds an ideal family — a notion based for the most part on nothing but sheer fantasy — in which everyone behaves nicely all or most of the time. If there is a great deal of bad behavior — answering back, refusing to obey, and/or sheer rebellion, bickering among siblings, muttering and mumbling, angry looks and gestures — many mothers actually believe that if only they were doing things right, all would be different.

Current studies of family living, more objective and much franker than in the past, paint a picture quite different from the over-idealized fantasy which many cling to. At least a certain amount of disharmony turns out to be not the exception, but the rule. And those families may be counted fortunate in which punishment does not elaborate into child abuse, and in which a certain amount of actual violence may not be the order of the day.

At any rate, certainly we all do our best. But it is very important for any disciplinarian to appreciate fully that some households are, by nature, more harmonious than others, some children infinitely easier to discipline than others.

The total household is a bit much for us to approach here, but we can make suggestions about different kinds of children and the kinds of discipline that may work best for each. Sometimes it seems almost easier for a mother if her first child is a tough one. There are some children who give difficulty seemingly almost from the moment they are conceived, and once born nothing seems really to work. If you have survived such a first, it can be all roses from then on. You may approach your second with apprehension, only to find that **whatever** you do works. If the reverse is true, and you have been lulled into a sense of false security by an easy first, an extremely difficult second may come as a most unwelcome surprise.

Having some idea about the differing kinds of discipline which work with different children may help. It is very important to keep in mind that there is no single approach, no one set of techniques, which work for everybody. Each child is different. Each child is special.

There are, for instance, some children with whom talking things out works wonders. You explain to them just what it was about their behavior which was wrong and which displeased you, ponder together about why they behaved as they did, make plans for a future in which you both could behave differently so that things would turn out better. If such a child questions an order or command, and you tell him that this particular request is **non-negotiable**, chances are he may then obey.

Some children **hate** those little talks and would much prefer a good, sharp slap (if you allow yourself such) to a discussion. Others **love** a good talk and, as they move on into the school years, may out-talk you to the point that you wish you had never started the conversation.

There are many children who, especially in the earlier years, react very well indeed to the well-known "time out" device. Time out may be spent in a special chair or, more likely, especially as children grow older, in their own room and stay there 'till the

timer rings. What magic they feel exists in the timer we have never figured out. But many almost unmanageable boys and girls will nevertheless wait until that timer does ring.

Some children seem born with the desire to please. Such children will often do something they do not want to do, or forego some pleasurable activity which they very much desire, just to make other people happy. Others seem almost spurred on to resistance, or to behavior which they know will get them into trouble, by expressions of disapproval on the part of the adult. It is almost as if, if they are already in trouble, this toughens them up. They know that if they keep on with whatever it is, the results will be disastrous, and it is almost as if they just don't care.

Another dichotomy lies between those children who need to be warned in advance that things are going to happen, and just how they will happen, and others who become tense and anxious about things if they are warned in advance. A parent soon appreciates that with such children you just have to spring things on them and hope for the best. Those who can accept advance warnings and be guided by them are, of course, the easier to deal with.

Thus there are little boys who can be told that tomorrow when they go to school (kindergarten or first grade), they are going to sit quietly in their seats, not wander about the room or the building, not talk too much in class, not talk back to the teacher, and when it is time to hand in their papers, they will hand them in and not insist (even though this may be the case) that they are not finished yet.

Or some children, if going to visit a relative, can be warned about the impending visit in advance and told in some detail, more or less, what is going to happen and how they will behave. Some mothers of rambunctious preschoolers even persuade their husbands to tell such children each morning just how they will behave throughout the day—all the good things they will do and the bad things they will refrain from doing. (Such a plan tends to work only in part, but some families have found it helpful.)

Another way in which children differ is in their reaction to scolding or punishment. There are some who say little, certainly do not cry, but may in reality be extremely sensitive to and influenced by what you say or do. You may really be getting through to them without realizing it.

Others may cry and carry on and swear that they will **never** do (whatever it was that they did wrong) again. You feel that you are really influencing them. However, if they are the kind of boy or girl who shows emotions easily but superficially, you may have hardly made a dent. And then there are those rough, tough boys who may seem almost to dare you to criticize or punish. With such boys or girls you may do your best to avoid direct or prolonged confrontation. Rather, after pointing out rather briefly what they have done that has not come up to standard, suggest for them some vigorous activity and then move rather quickly out of their orbit, to avoid a loud, exhausting scene.

Also, you might keep in mind that some children have a much more highly developed moral sense than others. Some children have extremely, even excessively, high standards for their own behavior. They do believe they should not even think bad thoughts. Others, especially those highly muscled individuals whom we describe as mesomorphs, often seem relatively unaware of subtle moral and ethical distinctions. They often need to be taught things that other children sense instinctively, things they just know they shouldn't do. Dr. William H. Sheldon has pointed out in his strong book, *Varieties of Delinquent Youth,* that the majority of delinquents he studied rated very high in mesomorphy, and that there were fewer delinquents among young men of other physical types.

Certainly no one special technique works with everybody. But we do maintain that if you follow our basic principle—know your child, understand as best you can the ways children of different personalities, at different ages, and in different situations customarily behave, and then adapt to this — whatever you child's personality, age or situation, things are more likely to go well, discipline is more likely to be effective, than if you just go ahead blindly, without understanding the child you are dealing with, and just assuming that some one method or technique will work for everybody, whatever the circumstances.

However, we have been speaking so far of children who, though they may at times be hard to manage, must be considered to be behaving well within normal limits. Not all children fall in this category. There are some who right from the beginning, even in infancy, are extremely difficult. Such children are described, and suggestions for disciplining them are provided in Dr. Stanley Turecki's excellent book, *The Difficult Child*. If you are at your wits' end in your efforts to get on with one of your children, we suggest this book.

According to Dr. Turecki, the child whom he describes as officially difficult has all or some of the following characteristics:

> He has a very high activity level. He gets wild, loses control, is excitable and impulsive.
>
> He is extremely distractable — has trouble paying attention, doesn't listen.
>
> He shows a high intensity — expresses his emotions loudly.
>
> His habits are irregular — it is hard to get him on a schedule.
>
> His initial impulse is to withdraw from whatever is offered.

He has a very low sensory threshold. Power struggles occur over clothes that don't "feel right," shoelaces that have to be retied endlessly, excessive sensitivity to noises, lights, smells, food tastes. Such a child can become hysterical over a minor cut or scrape.

He has terrible trouble with any transitions, any changes, anything different. And, unfortunately, is of a basically negative mood—sullen, cranky, unhappy, unpleasant. Prone to tears and tantrums.

You, obviously, already know most of this. But it may be helpful to appreciate that all of these things go together — they constitute the child's basic makeup. And there **are** things you can do to make matters better.

So what **do** you do if your son or daughter has turned out to be what Dr. Turecki designates as a "difficult child?" He suggests that to get discipline back in hand and to restore your rightful position of leadership in the family, you re-educate yourself to think in terms of your child's temperament, and then try to deal with **behavior** instead of responding emotionally or instinctively to what you perceive as his **motives**.

Before you can deal with any unsatisfactory behaviors effectively you need to adopt an objective attitude. The key issue is **neutrality**. Thus when your child misbehaves, don't respond emotionally, or instinctively. Instead, stand back and become as neutral as possible. Your response works best if it comes from your thinking and not your feeling.

Don't take what your child does personally. Don't ask yourself, "Why is he doing this to me?"

Any time you can relate a behavior to some aspect of your child's temperament, you will be in a better position to know what to do about it. Here are some guidelines to help you think about his behavior effectively:

Think about behaviors, not motivations. Concentrate on the fact that your child won't change her clothes, not that she won't do it because she wants her own way.

Get away from mere irritation and ask yourself, is the behavior really important?

Also ask yourself, are you being objective? How bad is the behavior in degree? And, does it occur often, or just now and then?

Don't concern yourself with projections into the future. Handle the **now**. Your child's personality when he grows up is not the issue. The issue is the situation right at hand.

Now, here are some clues that your disciplining may not be of the best. It probably isn't if you are screaming and yelling a lot, always saying "no," punishing more than you would like to, battling a lot, getting your child to promise that he will never do (whatever it is) again, threatening, punishing severely for something that really was not all that bad, feeling powerless, giving in a lot.

If these are your methods of punishment, you'll need to change them, and to concentrate not on feeling but on understanding the link between your child's behavior and his basically difficult temperament. But try to do that and try to remember that for the most part, your child is not being bad **on purpose**.

Punishment

Since many people, though we think incorrectly, identify discipline with punishment, a few words about punishment may be in order. Certainly many mothers, when they ask other mothers, "What do you find to be the most effective kind of discipline?" are really asking, "What is the best form of punishment?"

Ideally, if one's discipline were totally successful, there should be very little need for punishment. Unfortunately, with the best discipline in the world, the most well-adjusted parents and children, and the happiest homes one might imagine, things will still at times go wrong; most children will sometimes need to be punished.

However, if instead of identifying discipline with punishment, we think of punishment as something that happens when our discipline fails, hopefully this may reduce the amount of punishment that one hands out. That, perhaps, would be the first rule — try to keep punishment at a minimum.

A second rule might be, always ask yourself, what does this punishment which I am meting out teach my child? One of the formerly most common kinds of punishment, spanking, presumably does not teach a very useful lesson. It does teach that people bigger than we, if displeased, can hit us. This, of course, is not a very good lesson. And quite obviously as the child grows to be as big, or bigger than we, it is a rather dangerous lesson.

How about other of the more customary kinds of punishment? Time out, or "Go
to your room", nowadays is one of the more
favored punishments. This for many works out
very well and the lesson it presumably teaches
seems a reasonable one. It tells the child that if
he cannot behave in a reasonable way, he will
be separated from other people.

Taking away privileges, if not carried to extremes, seems
a reasonable and fair kind of punishment, and it teaches, if anything, that if you do not behave in an acceptable way, life will not go
smoothly for you.

Logical consequences have always seemed a sensible
kind of punishment. Your son leaves his bike out, though you had
instructed him to put it away, and somebody steals it. Result — he
has no bike to ride.

Scolding and speaking sharply, if not too intense or
prolonged, also seems to us a reasonable form of punishment. But
we are against yelling and the making of really violent threats. A
mother we know commented recently, "I'm so awful when I yell
that I wouldn't even listen to myself."

(In fact, angry as one may be at times, any kind of
punishment, administered calmly, tends to be much more effective
than one dealt out in rage.)

Some parents withhold the child's allowance as a preferred form of punishment. This to most, however, does not seem
fair. An allowance, when provided, is usually intended not as a
special reward or privilege. Rather the money is given as the child's
part of what the family has to provide. It probably is not a good idea
to tie it in with behavior, good or bad.

An occasional parent allows the child to choose his or her
own punishment. This could work, but it would require a fairly

reasonable and relatively mature child to make a good decision in such a case.

Whatever kind of punishment you choose, if you have told your child that the very next time he does (whatever it is that you don't like) you will punish in a certain way, do so. Do not keep stringing things out by going on and on with, "Now what did I tell you? And the very next time you do this, you are really going to get it." With such a parent, the child rather quickly learns that threats are meaningless.

To the extent that you can, if there is to be a punishment, it should come fairly soon after the incident for which the child is being punished. "Wait till your father comes home. Then you'll get it," is undesirable from two points of view. It makes Father into something of an ogre. And it strings out the unhappy situation. When things are unhappy and unpleasant, best to get punishment, if needed, over with as quickly as possible so as to clear the air.

No parent should feel guilty if now and then (oftener than that in the preschool years), a child has to be punished. But if punishment is the order of the day and something you depend on to keep things in hand, you would do well to review your method of disciplining. Ask yourself, "What could I do to make life go more smoothly in our household?"

Above all, if your boy or girl seems to be constantly in trouble, constantly doing bad or forbidden things which seem to require punishment, you might ask yourself, "Why does he behave so badly? Why does he seem almost to seek punishment?" Many of us feel that children who behave badly do so, at least part of the time, in order to get their parents' attention. To some children, negative attention and punishment are better than no attention at all. If this may be the case in your family, try going out of your way to see to it that your children do get attention from you when they do good things as well as bad.

Brothers and Sisters
Fighting

Since a very large proportion of home discipline problems have to do with the fact that brothers and sisters are always fighting, here are a few suggestions. Perhaps your most important tool in this respect is your own attitude. If you are one who believes that, as our grandmothers used to put it, aggravatingly, when **we** fought, "birds in their little nests agree," you are doomed to disappointment. On the other hand, if you are like the mother who once admitted, "Trying to stop my children from fighting would make no more sense than trying to stop them from breathing," you will be better prepared for what actually does happen in most families.

Children fight for many reasons. One is for territory. One or the other is in the way — sitting in your chair, usurping the telephone, monopolizing the television, breaking your toy, wearing your clothes, looking at your goldfish. Opportunities for irritation and annoyance are endless, even in a well-run, orderly and basically comfortable household.

They also fight for attention, and to be first in their parents' eyes. If parents are ignoring them, it is nearly always possible to get attention by starting a rousing fight. And if you can prove that a sibling did something wrong and can manage to get him or her punished, clearly **you** come out ahead. Rivalry between siblings is a basic and almost inevitable part of family living.

Much fighting is caused by the mere fact that children **enjoy** fighting with each other. This is a warm, strong, personal kind of activity. Siblings fighting with each other are really involved. This is real life.

Another reason children fight is because often they are mad at the world, unhappy with their lot, and they want to take things out on somebody. Safer to choose a younger sibling as a victim than some child outside the family or an adult.

Certainly, nobody could claim that all fighting between siblings is benign, and certainly most of us don't like to see it. But some psychiatrists, like Dr. Richard A. Gardner, in his lively and useful book, *Understanding Children*, go so far as to suggest that a fight a day keeps the psychiatrist away. Gardner feels that fighting between brothers and sisters is a manifestation of irrepressible, healthy forces within the child. In fact, he believes that any child who does not express at least some degree of sibling rivalry may be an inhibited child who has been defeated by those around him in the struggle for self-expression.

At any rate, that siblings will fight may be the first and most important notion to keep in mind when you are wondering how best to discipline your children when they fight with each other, as they inevitably will. Try not to hold yourself, and them, up to some impossible idea of family harmony. Face the fact, and accept it, that if there is more than one child in your household, there will be a good deal of fighting.

Several books have been written advising parents about ways to discipline their quarreling children, books including our own, *He Hit Me First*. In the interests of saving space, we here provide a brief list of Do's and another list of Don'ts with which parents may best handle the inevitable fighting and disagreement that goes on between brothers and sisters in an ordinary household.

Don'ts

Since it tends to be easier to tell people what **not** to do than what to do, we shall list some of the Don'ts that we and others have found useful in helping children in a family to get on with each other.

To begin with, **don't** act as a referee. At least don't do it any more than you inevitably will have to. What every child longs to hear is your verdict that "You were right and your brother (sister) was wrong" or "He was the one who started it. No wonder you hit him back." Try to avoid such definitive verdicts.

There will inevitably be times when you will be called upon to settle some dispute. Sometimes you can get out of it by saying, "You settle it yourselves." Or when some ill-doing on the part of a sibling is reported, you can say, "Well, what are you going to do about it?"

Don't intervene in normal bickering. If somebody is getting murdered, you will usually know it by the volume of the cries. (Or by the loudness of the silence.) The more you can manage to stay out of things, the more ingenious and self-reliant your children will become in settling their own squabbles.

Don't reward tattling by encouraging it.

Don't insist on getting to the bottom of things in the hope of finding out who was really to blame. There are rare instances when it is absolutely necessary for you to know how the whole thing started and who did what to whom. But much of the time, the whole story will be so convoluted, and often only slightly related to the truth of the matter, and each of two or three combatants will be so dedicated to proving that he or she was the innocent victim, that even the most skilled efforts cannot reveal the true facts.

Most fighting between siblings has long and tangled roots. The one who seems on the surface to have started it may actually be the victim of a clever conniver. He messed up her paper dolls, it may be true. But she swiped his bubble gum first. And before that, he bothered her when she and her friends were playing house. (Et cetera, et cetera, et cetera.)

Also, any formal inquisition achieves just the result you were trying to avoid. It attracts your attention, takes your time and encourages your children in the hope of achieving victory over an (often) hated rival.

Thus, **don't** allow your children to draw you into a pattern of spending a vast amount of time and energy discussing and trying to straighten out their disagreements. Keep any such sessions as few and brief as possible.

Don't set yourself up by allowing repetition of situations which you know aren't going to work. For instance, if your Six-year-old, like most, absolutely cannot stand to lose a competitive game, don't permit him to play such games with, let's say, a demanding Eight-year-old. Or not often, anyway. Fighting, blaming, and name calling is almost certain to result.

Don't bemoan loudly, often, and in the children's presence that they fight all the time and you just cannot stand it or do anything about it. Most children are ready and eager to live up to such advance billing. Keep your anxieties to yourself and try to do something about the quarreling. Any child in any family is likely to feel that his parents always favor the other(s). This can't be helped. **Don't** add fuel to the fire by allowing yourself to favor one or the other conspicuously, even though your heart may urge you to do so. You very likely **will** have a favorite, but try not to make this grossly obvious.

In fact, **don't**, at least in their presence, compare your children to each other. Don't hold one up as an example to the other(s): "Why can't you mind what I say the way your sister does?"

Don't go on and on about some misbehavior which is now safely in the past.

Don't allow your children to play you against your spouse. In all likelihood, one of you will be a little more lenient, one a little more strict, than the other. This is natural and not necessarily harmful. But do your best not to let the children capitalize on it or use it to gain favors. Do your best to back each other up. If you can't manage this, perhaps one could have charge of certain activities, and one of others.

If you are the homebound parent, **don't** take all the blame for the way the children behave. Though many children do behave a little better for their father than their mother (they are usually more afraid of him), if he feels that you are doing a lousy job with them and their bickering, arrange that he be the person in charge, at least for a while.

(However, unless the problem is horrendous, don't say, "Wait till your father comes home and he will settle things." Try to handle problems at the time at which they occur. Not at the end of the day.)

Don't set unrealistic goals with regard to the degree of family harmony that you expect. Start where you actually are and then try, little by little, to improve matters.

Don't allow yourself to over-identify. For instance, try to avoid over-identifying with your poor, darling daughter who is always being picked on by her mean, big brother. If anything can cloud a clear evaluation of a present situation, it can be an over-identification with your own past.

Do's

And now for the Do's. To begin with, **do** keep in mind that most children fight. A lot.

Although we've warned you not to try to get to the bottom of every quarrel, **do** try to find out why your children fight. The reasons may be so deep-seated—basic hatred, desperate jealousy—that they will be hard to deal with. But the reason sometimes might be a small or specific thing that you could do something about.

Try making **need** rather than **fairness** the basis for decisions. Things never do come out entirely fairly, and even if they did, the children wouldn't think so. So get whatever it is for the child who needs it, not for every child in the family.

Do avoid situations that, by their very nature, will cause difficulty. If two boys under four have each a box of pennies, each is bound to believe that the other has some of **his** pennies.

Do separate your children more than you may be doing. Break up bad combinations so far as you reasonably can.

Do use **rules**. Many children, especially preschoolers, tend to be absolutely snowed if you tell them that something is "the rule." To make this work, make rules simple and specific. Avoid big, general rules, such as "You must be good to your sister." Instead, state specifically, "The rule is that you must not hit your sister."

Do what you can to make each child feel special. Spend as much time alone with each as you possibly can. And **do** help children protect their most prized possessions. You can't keep siblings from **looking** at them, but at least do all you can to keep a child's very best things from being destroyed.

Do try to help your child find varied outlets for emotions, so that fighting with siblings will not be the primary pleasure.

Do encourage children to work out their own solutions— unless of course the two in question are vastly ill matched.

If you know that a certain kind of situation always turns out badly, but that situation cannot be avoided entirely, try to step in before the lid blows off.

Try using Behavior Modification techniques. That is, reward behavior that you wish to have repeated. So far as you reasonably can, ignore the bad.

Do all you can to reduce tattling by making it unrewarding.

Do on occasion try role playing or role reversal. Thus, let a younger child play the role of an older child and vice versa. This can, on occasion, be both entertaining and effective.

When the quarreling and fighting in the household seem to have reached extremes, here's a trick that some find helpful. Keep a diary, list or chart—anything that will objectify the situation. This device can give you a realistic picture of just how bad (or good) things really are. A chart could show you just how long, or under what circumstances, your children actually can play nicely together. Knowing what the pattern actually is can sometimes help you know what to avoid. Often it can also cheer you up by showing that things in your household are much better than you had feared.

If children are very angry at each other, just telling them not to hit or hurt each other does little to defuse their anger. This may sound rather quirky, but some parents find it works well to suggest to two sibs who are fighting that each draw the ugliest picture possible of the other. This serves two purposes. It tells them that you understand they **are** angry at each other, and it gives them a chance to vent their anger in an acceptable manner.

If things are really horrendous in your household, **do** feel free to get outside help. Family therapy has saved many families' sanity. And for yourself, take some time off from your children each day—certainly each week. Anything looks better if you can get away from it, even briefly.

Discipline In Nursery School and Day Care

Now that an increasing number of children under kindergarten age are spending substantial time during their early years in nursery schools or day care, discipline in these situations can be almost as big a problem as discipline at home. Experienced nursery school teachers themselves have much to tell the rest of us about this matter, but for beginning teachers, or for day care providers who have not had formal training in the care of the young, the following suggestions may be of use.

Adjusting the Child to School

This may to some not seem to be a disciplinary problem, but actually much discipline may be involved. And certainly the very first thing one has to do in either school or a day care center is to separate the child from his mother or other, get him into the building, and get him started in some more or less happy play or other activity.

Infants and others under Eighteen months of age may be easier to adjust to the new scene or person than those just older. Possibly the Eighteen-monther, Two-year-old and Two-and-a-half-year-old have the hardest time. Two, especially, feels very close to his mother, and since he tends to be shy of new people and new places, he is not particularly ready for new adventures. If the child clings too tightly to his mother (or his mother clings too tightly to him), it may work out best to have someone other than Mother bring him to school. Most children of these ages separate much more easily from their fathers, for instance, than from their mothers.

Whoever brings him, one special teacher (preferably the same one every day) should be right on hand to greet him, and to distract him from the pain of parting by suggesting something they can do together. As for instance, "Let's go find the bunny." Weather permitting, this transition from mother to teacher often works best out of doors than indoors. Though it helps right away to suggest some attractive activity, it is the person of the teacher which really matters. Children under three are not always too enthusiastic about the other children in the group but most, once adapted, love the teacher.

Things shift by Three to Three-and-a-half. Now the other children tend to be of more interest than any adults who may be present. So, if the child is still making a fuss about parting from the person who brings him, a statement such as, "Your friend, Jennifer (or Joe), is waiting for you in the doll corner," will usually help even a rather reluctant girl or boy to part from parents and mingle with the group.

Something which can be of consolation to any parent whose child weeps and clings at the moment of parting is the fact that nearly all children, once Mother has departed, adapt very happily to the group situation and do not cry or fuss again — if at all — until she returns.

Helping the Child Get on with Other Children

Discipline, in many nursery schools and day care centers as in many households, often is primarily related to the way children get on with each other. In school, if you ask the children to sit down to have milk and crackers, usually they obey. If you say it's time to go outdoors, few resist. But when it comes to getting on with the other children, here very often serious and strenuous problems arise. A good clear knowledge of the way young children relate to each other at the several preschool ages can go a long way to helping a teacher or day care worker see to it that child-child relations are harmonious and happy.

Eighteen Months

At Eighteen months of age, most boys and girls are not particularly interested in other children, except perhaps as objects which they can explore. A child may poke another child's eyes, pull at his hair — or may in fact grab an object from another child with virtually no attention to this other child. This behavior is not unfriendly or hostile. It is simply that Eighteen-monthers are not much interested in other children. Though nowadays many children of this age do need to be in day care centers, this is not an ideal age for nursery school, assuming that a family can provide care for their child in other ways.

Two Years

Even by Two years of age, there tends to be relatively little interaction between or among children. Many look at other children, occasionally speak to them, but there tends to be neither much cooperation or much fighting. About the most that the majority do in relation to other children is to engage in what is called parallel play. That is, two children may stand beside each other at the sand box or clay table but, for the most part, each will be engaged in his or her own solitary play.

Two-and-a-half Years

It is especially around Two-and-a-half years of age that teachers or other caretakers can be helped in their disciplining by an understanding of what children are like at this time in their lives. The average Two-and-a-half-year-old wants complete possession of any toy or other object that he or she is playing with, has played with, or might later wish to play with. Thus, any child holding or touching any object whatsoever constitutes a threat.

Understanding this will help you not to think of the child as grabby, selfish, unreasonable. It should certainly prevent you from even thinking of punishing a child who behaves in this way. It should encourage you to use some of the techniques which have been found to work so well at this clearly rather selfish age.

Thus, if two children are fighting over a train, you can ask, "What else could Johnny use? Let's find him a truck." You can say, "Pretty soon it will be his turn to play with the train." You can say — and it is surprising to note how often this transparent ruse actually works, "But Johnny needs the train."

(Whatever the problem, there are certain words or phrases which do seem to work like magic: "Needs," "Has to have," "When he's finished," "Its time to," "Oh, you forgot.")

Even simpler, you can provide at least two of most things, though even this is not going to end all squabbling. Also, do not, as an adult, feel that all disputes need to be settled fairly. Sometimes, in the interests of getting on with things, it has to end up that a more demanding or grabby child gets his way at the expense of a gentler one. Above all, try not to make a big deal of this kind of situation. Remain casual and calm. Don't let the child think that the solution of a struggle is of vast importance to the adult.

Three Years

By Three, to a large extent, children have moved away from their primary preoccupation with the teacher (or other adults), and from their excessive need to possess any object available, to an interest in and concern about other children. If you are lucky, many children actually want things to go well for them and their friends. "We" is an important word to them. So, in any group situation, the child may be his or her own best disciplinarian, behaving in a way that will make things nice for all concerned.

Three-and-a-half Years

Though inclusion may be the theme at Three, for many, exclusion may be the theme at Three-and-a-half. This is a tricky, tenuous, uncertain, troubled age at best. For many children, interpersonal relations by no means always go smoothly. Much social interaction is interfered with by statements of, "You can't play with us," "We don't like you," "Stay away." At such times, moralistic comments by the teacher to the effect that that is not a nice way to talk or act fall on deaf ears, or merely solidify the in-group.

Best to handle such situations lightly with practical explanations, such as, "He could be the mailman bringing the mail," "She could be the grandmother coming to visit." Or take their minds off excluding by asking some question such as, "Do you want her to bring you some bread or some butter?" Or if children remain implacable, the teacher herself can join the play group, bringing with her, without comment, the excluded child.

Any such simple techniques tend to work wonders. Many at this age do not exclude another child because they really don't like him. They tend to exclude for the sheer pleasure of excluding. Given a good excuse to include, they may do that just as easily.

Four Years

Discipline having to do with relationships with other children, by Four, is much less needed than earlier. Children use their own techniques on each other: "May I please have my iron now?" "It's my turn now. OK?" The game is the thing, and many show real maturity in handling their relationships with others. Your main disciplinary problems at this age, if one so considers them, are the child's tendency to boasting, bragging, prevaricating, swearing, and excessive use of bathroom language. Since nearly all these things are done for effect, the calmer one remains, the less attention one pays to such comments as, "You old poo-poo face", the sooner the child will desist.

Transitions

Transitions, either at home or at school, tend to be among the things most difficult for young children. They tend to cause the most difficulty, the most resistance, the most rebellion and the least compliance. Thus, as much as anything else, it is during transition times that some sort of disciplinary action is often required. As different as each child may be from every other, nevertheless there are many, many things which all at any age seem to have in common. We have found through the years that there are many simple techniques for making transitions go smoothly — techniques which work more often than one might anticipate. Here are some which we have found most useful.

Two Years

Two tends to dawdle. Likes to keep on with what he is doing. Hates to shift. Thus try:

1. Leading him away by the hand, if he doesn't resist too strongly. (You can give a little tug if he resists initially.)

2. Tell him to say goodbye to whatever he is doing, i.e., "Say goodbye to the sand table."

3. Talking about the new thing you wish him to do: "Let's go find the soap."

4. Lure him by holding out some enticing toy.

5. As at Eighteen months, you can just go up behind him, pick him up bodily without comment, and put him where you want him to be.

6. If he is one who seems to need advance notice, you can warn him with such a remark as, "Pretty soon we'll go to the bathroom and then we'll have juice."

Perhaps the most important thing, at this age or at any other, is your attitude. Children are impressed by a calm, firm attitude which implies an assurance on your part that they are going to comply with your wishes or requests. Any uncertainty on your part will be noted immediately. Especially avoid any question which could easily be answered by "No," as, "Do you want to do so and so?"

Two-and-a-half Years

This being an especially perseverative age, transitions may be harder than ever. So you must expect a slow adjustment to new materials or new situations, a strong holding on to the old, and a very slow release even after interest has actually waned.

No, I won't.

You get farther in helping a child move on to something new if you try not to make too much of an issue of it, if you do not hurry the child too much. If you have been fortunate enough to set up rituals which work ("After we do this, we then do that"), even though they may take extra time, make use of them.

When it comes time to leave with Mother, children at this age may make a big fuss. They either don't want to leave at all, insist on "just one more turn," or may even try to hide. Mothers should be helped to appreciate that this is customary behavior and not a rejection of them as persons.

Three Years

This tends to be an easy-going, relatively compliant age. Many Threes quite willingly will leave, even something they are vastly enjoying, to do something else which a teacher suggests. Should there be mild resistance, as to going to the bathroom or to stop individual play in order to take part in some group routine in another part of the room, it sometimes works to suggest new ways of going from one place to another — as to run, jump, hop to the place or situation in question.

Three-and-a-half Years

Children of this age tend not to be to easy to handle, and mature as they are (compared to what has gone before), many are not only rather guileful, but extremely determined to do things their own way and with their own timing. If they don't want to do something when and as you want them to, they will make this all too evident. Thus, considerable skill and subtlety are needed, on the part of the adult, if things are to go as the adult wishes them to.

A Three-and-a-half-year-old may balk with a strong "No, I don't want to," with argument, or even with tears and wailing when even some rather simple and usual move is suggested. Sometimes a teacher can take the child by surprise, and override his objections simply by saying something like "Scat." Or she may think of some good and clever reason why the child should do as she suggests. However, just because something works one day is no guarantee that it will the next.

One of the best ways of obtaining compliance at this age is not to stay and fight things out on the child's own ground, but to change the subject or situation entirely. Talk about something else. Children now are also extremely vulnerable to compliments about their appearance or good behavior. A compliment about their shoes, socks, or any article of their apparel, will often distract them from whatever it was they were holding on to or refusing to do, and before you know it, they will be doing what you had in mind.

Four Years

Happily, at this age and from now on, transitions tend not to be the big deal they were earlier. Since this is an age where tricks are enjoyed, somewhat as earlier, one can suggest new ways of moving on to another kind of play or other part of the room. One can encourage them to hop or skip instead of merely walking or running.

Their new interest in numbers, also, can be used as a motivating technique: "Let's see if you can do it before I count to ten." Or the clock can be used: "When the big hand gets to eleven, you may get up."

Competition with people as well as with time is sometimes stimulating: "See if you can beat me back into the house." And, as earlier, praise and compliments usually work nicely. If you compliment them for something they have done well in the past (and hopefully are going to do well right now), it is often hard for them to refuse to do it.

Individual problems of discipline can arise at any age, but Fours as a group, though they often need toning down, do not get their backs up as much as younger children. If things go well, they tend to be both amused and amusing.

Verbal vs. Physical Handling

Eighteen Months

This is the chief age at which physical handling may be equally effective as verbal in getting children to do what one wishes—which is, after all, perhaps the main goal of good discipline. Just the right words, if kept very simple and clear — "Go out," "Coat off," "Cookie," often are sufficient to direct the child to the activity or object which you have in mind.

However, words are not always needed. It can often be quite successful, if you want an Eighteen-monther to be in some part of the room other than where he may be at the moment, simply to go up behind him and without comment, lift him and carry him to the other spot.

Less direct but usually effective can be such tricks as holding out to the child a favorite toy or beloved stuffed animal. Chances are very good that he will come to you (which has presumably been what you had in mind) in order to obtain this object. You don't have to talk about it, don't need to say, "Come here."

Two Years

Now verbal handling is beginning to work better than physical handling. A Two-year-old might very well object to being picked up and placed elsewhere. But words, if well chosen, will often do the trick. It is important to keep language simple, concrete, and repetitive. There is no need to fear boring the Two-year-old with repetition. The world is all so new to him that repetition helps make him feel secure.

But, keep language at a minimum. The adult who talks too much to the Two-year-old soon loses his attention, and also is in danger of using words the child does not understand.

The adult's language should be modeled on the level of the children. Typical useful phrases are: "Have clay after juice," "When it's time," "This is where it fits." Emphasize important words with a calm, reassuring tone. Your tone and manner are probably more important than your actual words.

Often it is necessary to follow or support your words with action. Thus, rather than simply saying, "Go wash your hands," a teacher may need to lead the child to the washbasin or sink. (Also try to get the child himself to substitute words for action. Try saying, "Jane can talk to Jimmy. Jane, say 'No' to Jimmy.")

Keep in mind that Two is not ready for sophisticated language or even for modest generalizations. Thus, instead of saying, "Let's put the toys away," try "Your dolly goes in the bed." And though you may not need to move the child physically, you may need to use physical gestures to make clear the meaning of your words.

Two-and-a-half Years

Now words are really coming into their own as motivators. If well chosen, and especially if they are familiar words, they can work like magic. As mentioned earlier, they can do wonders in getting children of this age to share — something they do at best only reluctantly. "Needs," "Has to have," "When he's finished," "It's time to," are all useful phrases.

Questions, also, are useful. Instead of giving the child a direct command, which may cause him to balk, try a question such as, "What do you do with your cup?", "Where does your coat go?" (Avoid any question that can be answered by "No.")

Ritualistic repetition of words and phrases often will smooth the way to some change of pace, some new activity: "Now we put the blocks away," "Now it's milk and cracker time."

Three Years

Now, as so often, things are changing. Just the right use of words can still act like magic, but now instead of preferring the familiar, children love the new and different. Language is really flowering. Try any of the following:

1. Key adjectives — "new," "different," "big," "strong." "Could

you make a different kind?" — stimulate the child within a situation without giving him a specific idea. "Can you carry two big ones?" may be the needed challenge to put the blocks away.

2. Key nouns — "surprise," "secret," "When you finish going to the bathroom I have a surprise for you," may organize a scraggly group.

3. Key verbs — "help," "might," "could," "Guess what," "needs." "You could help John fill the cart," may produce not only the desired action but also the satisfaction as expressed in "I'm helping."

4. Key adverbs — "maybe," "how about," "too." "You could help, too," helps the child to join in the group activity.

The Three-year-old — unlike his earlier self — often listens well when he is reasoned with. He may even do things he does not like to do if given a good reason, as for instance, "Let's pick up the blocks so we'll have room to dance." The use of "maybe," "you might," "perhaps," "you could," gives the child a chance to back out gracefully if the demand is really too much. It also gives the adult a graceful exit, if the child objects to what you have asked and you do not have the strength or interest to pursue the matter.

However, important and exciting as words tend to be to the average Three-year-old, now and even later the adult may, on occasion, need to go back to plain physical handling.

Three-and-a-half Years

Even more than just earlier, this is a sociable, "me, too" age. A skillful adult can put to good advantage the fact that children like to imitate. Since they will imitate the undesirable as well as the desirable, it is best to emphasize the right way to do things rather than commenting on what you may consider the wrong way.

Because of their "me, too" tendency, once you get a leader going in the right direction, the rest may very well follow.

Since many are moving on toward the noisy rowdiness of Four, part of an adult's job will be to keep the lid on things. Sometimes this can be done by whispering. Many will stop what they are doing in order to hear a whispered command or suggestion.

The element of surprise, as well as a love of the new and different, can be strong motivators. "Do you know what?" is a question which can interrupt the child's actions (if he is doing something you don't very much like), and can make him receptive to your new suggestion. If you tell a child that something you propose is "new," "different," "special," "exciting," chances are he will believe you.

And, as at other ages, once words have come in with strong importance, praise and compliments can be effective motivators. As can the use of the word "friend." You can really soften the child up by telling him that he is your friend. Or you can often make him accept another child whom he may not especially like by telling him that the child is his friend.

Since this is a high point for imaginary companions, many children vary this by liking to be called by names other than their own. If you can hit on the child's favorite make-believe name, you can often motivate him to good behavior far beyond what may be usual for him. Try things like, "And now Mickey Mouse does so and so," or "Come on, Kitten, let's pick up the blocks."

Or, when other activities pale, just having a nice conversation with the child of this age can give both adult and child a good deal of pleasure.

Four Years

Key words used by the adult for Three-and-a-half-year-olds, such as "different," "surprise," "guess," etc. are now in the verbal repertoire of the child and are used spontaneously, but he still responds to the adult use of them. However, his own use of language is so adequate that he dos not respond as markedly to key words as earlier. One's manner of handling is now more important than the actual words used. The child may respond best to a man-to-man attitude in conversation.

The Four-year-old demands reasons with "Why?" and "How?" and frequently can be answered by turning a question back to him. Whispering is still as effective as at Three-and-a-half.

Children of this age enjoy new, different, and big words. They use and like exaggeration: "As high as the sky," "In a hundred years." This exaggeration often leads to the telling of tall stories, which should be enjoyed momentarily by adult and child, and then should be brought into perspective by pointing out the difference between real and imaginary.

Five Years and After

Five-year-olds are, in general, so very much more mature than Fours in their response to adults that simple verbal techniques no longer can be expected to work the miracle they sometimes do at earlier ages. Now you are more or less on your own, with the individual child and the particular situation. General suggestions for getting on with Five-year-olds can be found in earlier sections.

Typical Activity Patterns of Preschoolers

Our position, throughout this book, is that the more one knows about what children are really like, the more effectively we can interact with them, and thus the more effective our discipline will be. One important characteristic of very young children, and one which changes rapidly with age, is their amount of physical activity. We have checked, in our own nursery school, to determine the amount of moving about the room characteristic of children at Eighteen months, Two years, Three years and Four years of age.

As Figure 3 makes clear, this amount decreases in almost startling fashion through this short age span. A typical Eighteen-monther is constantly on the go. He seems almost to think with his feet. Instead of determining some certain goal and then aiming for it, he seems often to be in almost constant movement. Two, somewhat less mobile, appears to have determined goals, and moves back and forth from one to the other, staying only very briefly in any one spot. The Two-and-a-half-year-old, and increasingly the child of Three, moves to some area of interest and remains there often for several minutes at a time. Four will often spend five or more minutes in some certain spot engaged in some chosen activity.

Clearly, the longer the child remains in one place, the more opportunity for favorable communication between him and the adult or adults available. The Eighteen-monther is like mercury. He slips through your fingers even as you try to grasp him. His sometimes almost constant movement offers little opportunity for discussion or discipline. Four is quite something else again.

NURSERY SCHOOL TECHNIQUES

YEARS	VERBAL TECHNIQUES	ADJUSTING CHILDREN AT ARRIVAL	DRESSING	UNDRESSING	TOILETING
2	Words work better than physical force, which wasn't so at 18 months. Use few words, keep them simple, and repeat them. It may help to follow words with action. A Two doesn't listen to or understand much adult talk. At Two—but not later —safe to ask specific "Do you want" questions. Responds well to physical and verbal affection.	Personal contact with teacher helpful. Take hand and talk to child as he or she arrives. Some like to hear same words or be greeted by name each day. Parting from caregiver often not difficult.	Keep children in one room while dressing them. At Two they don't like to help selves. But amount of self-help may vary with child and from day to day. Many are better at taking off than putting on, but teacher must do most. Ones who help selves, even a little, should be praised. Dress most aggressive and noisy first and have aide take outside. Label clothes and keep in proper cubbies.	Undressing works best if child is held on lap and clothes removed without child's help. At Two usually no resistance.	Generally unaware. If training started at home, it may continue at school. Don't press matter if child resists. Training pants are easily changed. Commenting when changing pants may create interest in toileting. Look for readiness signs and take child to bathroom on some excuse to see others functioning.
2½	Questions are helpful to get children to act, but avoid those that can be answered "No." Avoid commands and choices except in unimportant things. Words still need to be backed up with action. Don't use big words. Praise works well.	Child may object to almost anything. Finds change hard, so doesn't like to leave caregiver and accept teacher and school. Give child interesting task or special routine to do right away.		Tends to run around. Doesn't want clothes taken off. Dislikes changes and tends to resist anything adults want. Hanging things up needs supervision.	About half may not be able to tell needs, but others can ask for toileting. Only a few have accidents. Some may not care and it's useless to try with them. With others, try carrying child to bathroom while talking about something else, but if child resists, give up the idea.

3	No longer need to repeat or say just right thing, but some special words work very well to get children to act. Positive, specific statements work best. Continue to avoid questions that can be answered "No." Humor often gets child to do what is asked. If child says "No, no, no," try "Yes, yes, yes."	Most adjust much better than earlier. Eager to come to school. May get out of car or bus and come in by self. Children should be greeted personally.		So eager to play, all insist on being undressed at once. Some would play inside without removing outside clothing. Unsnap and unzip a few to start group. Urge them to try themselves. Some may help each other, which isn't too helpful but keeps them busy. Still very little interest in hanging up clothes.	Most are toilet trained. They tell teacher when they're going to ask for help if needed. Routine toileting is needed for younger children in group. As at Two, may object to toileting at school, especially during the first few weeks. Such refusal should be respected.
4	Praise and compliments continue as best techniques. Praise child's good relations with others. Positive approach still best, but negative one may also work. Other children's feelings, or why things should or shouldn't be done, should be explained. Children love humor and respond well to exaggeration and silly talk.	More mature, more individual approval needed for each child. They still like warm, personal greeting. If there's trouble leaving caregiver, talk it over or plan ahead of time for child to bring something special to share with group.	All can help selves. Some dress selves entirely. Enough space should be available to avoid fights. Putting clothes in piles around room works best. Have each child dress by own pile. Praise independent ones; others may imitate.	In a hurry to have things taken off/interesting activity coming up. Many manage by selves. If help is needed, teacher should give it. If child resists, ignore it and talk of something else while helping.	

Accomplishments and Abilities

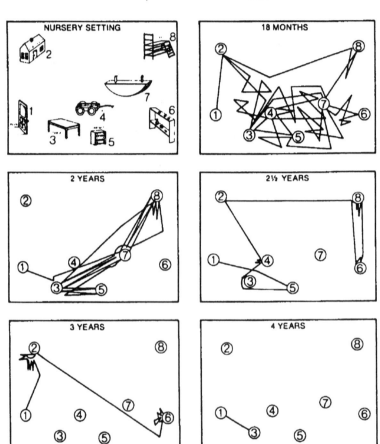

Figure 3
*Seven Clocked Minutes of Nursery School
Behavior at Different Ages*

Conclusion

In summary, may we suggest that all of you parents or teachers who are dealing with young children just do the best you can. Adopt a concept, or philosophy, of discipline, a practice of discipline, which comes natural to you and with which you, yourself, feel comfortable.

Though there is much that is alike from child to child, and many methods of discipline that seem to work for almost anybody, every child is unique, every parent is unique, every family is unique. More than that, the kind of discipline that may be very effective at some one age may be totally inappropriate at another.

All of this most certainly means that you cannot find some bit of advice offered by some certain child specialist, apply it to your own situation, and find that you are home free. Disciplining is always a matter of trial and error, and it goes on nearly all the time, except when your children are asleep. (And it may very likely have taken a certain amount of discipline to get them to sleep.)

Perhaps our most important message about all this is to try to relax. Do not expect perfection. Do not expect the impossible from yourself or from your children. Emotions between parent and child tend to run very high. The strength of even a very young child's feelings as he fights tooth and nail to get his own way tends to surprise us. And your own feelings tend to be strong as you struggle to make your child behave as you feel he ought to do, for his own good.

One of the chief tasks of childhood is to get free of one's family, to stand on one's own feet. But this freeing oneself from parental control and domination is not achieved comfortably or easily. It comes, in most, through a series of tears and tantrums, of tugs and pulls, or straining at the leash and then repeatedly settling back into the comfort of doing what your parents want you to do.

It is important for parents to keep in mind that, when the child may seem to be behaving his worst, that this may be the very time when he needs the most from you — the most acceptance, the most appreciation, the most affection.

So, try to stay calm. Try to take a long-term view. Try to see any momentary struggle or conflict as perhaps a mere milestone on the long path of your relationship with this young person, who means so much to you and to whom you are, at least in his early years, the all-powerful arbiter of his life and destiny.

References

Ames, Louise B.; Ilg, Frances L. and Sidney M. Baker *Your Ten- to Fourteen-Year-Old*. New York: Delacorte, 1988.

Bayard, Robert T. and Jean Bayard. *How to Deal With Your Acting-Up Teenager: Practical Self-Help for Desperate Parents*. New York: M. Evans & Co., Inc., 1983.

Dinkmeyer, Don. *Parenting Your Child*. Circle Pines, Minnesota: American Guidance Press, 1989.

Dodson, Fitzhugh. *How to Discipline With Love*. New York: Rawson, 1977.

Gardner, Richard A. *Understanding Children*. New York: Aronson, 1974.

Gesell, Arnold; Ilg, Frances L.; Ames, Louise B.; and Janet Learned Rodell. *Infant And Child In The Culture Of Today*. Rev. Ed. New York: Harper and Row, 1974.

Graubard, Paul S. *Positive Parenthood*. New York: Bobbs Merill, 1977.

Grisanti, Mary Lee; Smith, Dian G.; and Charles Flatter. *Parents' Guide To Understanding Discipline*. Englewood Cliffs, New Jersey: Prentice Hall, 1990.

Matthews, Sanford J. *Through The Motherhood Maze*. New York: Doubleday, 1982.

Procaccinni, Joseph and Mark W. Kiefaber. *P.L.U.S. Parenting: Take Charge of Your Family*. New York: Doubleday, 1989.

Sheldon, William H. *Varieties of Delinquent Youth*. New York: Harper & Row, 1949.

Turecki, Stanley and Leslie Tonner. *The Difficult Child*. New York: Bantam, 1985.

Wood, Paul and Bernard Schwartz. *How to Get Your Children to Do What You Want Them to Do*. Englewood Cliffs, New Jersey: Prentice Hall, 1978.

York, Phyllis; York, David and Ted Wacthel. *Toughlove*. Garden City, New York: Doubleday, 1982.

Zinsser, Caroline. "The Discipline Debate: Is There a Right Way to Say 'Knock it Off?'" in *The Working Mother*. July, 1983, pp. 60-61.